SHALL WE TITHE?

"Study to shew thyself approved unto God"

II Timothy 2:15

Michael O. Coman

ISBN 0-7414-3131-9

Published by:

INFINITY
PUBLISHING.COM

1094 New DeHaven Street, Suite 100
West Conshohocken, PA 19428-2713
Info@buybooksontheweb.com
www.buybooksontheweb.com
Toll-free (877) BUY BOOK
Local Phone (610) 941-9999
Fax (610) 941-9959

Printed in the United States of America

Printed on Recycled Paper

Published July 2006

SHALL WE TITHE?

Table of Contents

Preface

SHALL WE TITHE?

When I accepted salvation, I wanted to do everything that God commanded us to do. One of the first things that I was instructed to do was to Tithe. I was told that tithing was something I must do in order to be obedient to God's Word— as well as to receive his blessings! Mostly, I wanted to be in total obedience to God's Word, so tithing became a part of my Christian life.

Throughout the years as I grew in Christ, I started to see things in the Word that were contrary to my teachings. When I would ask other believers about the differences between the Word and their teachings, most felt the same as I did. But no one ever stopped to ask any questions such as; why didn't Jesus teach the Disciples to do it? Jesus did say in the "Great Commission," "Teaching them to observe all things whatsoever I have commanded you" (Mat 28:19-20). Or why is it not preached on and taught on besides just quoting one or two Scriptures from the book of Malachi? Most people in the Body of Christ are not even aware of the fact that the Tithe was the source for the Blood Sacrifices (Numbers 18:1-17)! Oh do I have your attention now? But in church, the only thing I ever heard coming out of the pulpit was, "It's in the Bible; God said it, so we have to do it, and if we don't, then we are cursed with a curse!" So I asked myself, is this threat of being under a curse the reason why we Tithe? Well, in order to answer that question, I had to reason with myself. You mean the curse mentioned in the book of Malachi? The same curse that came from the curses proclaimed over the Children of Israel under the Law of Moses (Deut 27:11/28:23)? The same curse from the LAW that is the very judgment for not obeying all of the works of

i

the Law? (Deut 27:26/Gal 3:10) A curse from the LAW that Jesus himself has already become for us? (Galatians 3:13) No, justifying the tithe based on this curse would not make any sense, now would it? So then I asked myself, do we Tithe because of the fact that Abraham started it? Well, if this is true, then I suppose we should still circumcise, for religious reasons, considering Abraham started this as well. Is Abraham superior to Christ? Of course not! In the book of Hebrews 2:1, we see it is the teachings of Christ that we are to adhere to and not to practice those of old. So then how could we, as followers of Christ, practice a commandment that was clearly under the Law, when we are under Grace (Hebrews 7:5/Galatians 5:4)?

I will tell you why, by using this curse as a scare tactic, the Tithe will bring a substantial amount of money into the different churches, and people will not even attempt to question it! Well, without the asking of questions, there would be no understanding of God's Word. God doesn't want his people to be afraid of his word. This is why Jesus told us to "Seek and ye shall find." After studying and researching God's Word, with the help of the precious Holy Spirit, there have been some things enlightened in my life. This is not a new type of Theology or denominational practice; this is the Word of God that has been overlooked, for whatever reason in the hearts of men. I would like to share these revelations, with the Body of Christ.

As you read the words in this book, I pray for the Holy Spirit to prepare your heart so that this seed will land on good ground. Make sure that you have your Bible to follow along and take your time so that this seed can take root. We have been blinded by the enemy for far too long! It is time for the Body of Christ to stop proclaiming curses from the Law over ourselves so that we can truly begin to recognize and receive God's blessings!

Therefore, you shepherds, hear the word of the lord.

Ezekiel 34:7

Chapter One

HISTORY OF THE TITHE

"What Was the Tithe?"

The first Tithe recorded in the Bible was when Abram (Abraham) returned from a battle with Ched-or-la-o-mer King of E-lam; he was greeted by the High Priest of God, Mel-chiz-e-dek, whom blessed Abram and God. Abram, being a man of God, gave the High Priest tithes, or ten percent of all that he had taken in the battle. Thus, we see the initial giving of a tenth of a possession, which continued on throughout the Old Testament. In chapter 28 of the book of Genesis, verse 11 through 22, Jacob, the son of Isaac, said to the Lord that if God would take care of him and allow him to make it safely unto his father's house in peace, that he would serve God and give him a tenth of all that God had given him. This was the last account of tithing until God gave the Children of Israel his commandments through their leader Moses.

In Leviticus chapter 27, verse 30, Moses tells the Children of Israel that all of the tithe of the land, whether of the seed of the land or of the fruit of the tree, it is the Lord's; it is holy unto the Lord. Even the tithe of the land or of the flocks even of whatsoever passeth under the rod, the tenth shall be holy unto the Lord. Moses gave the Children of Israel a vivid picture of how serious the tenth of everything that God blessed them with was, but there was one thing missing: what did God want them to do with it? Well, before we discuss how God instructed the Children of Israel to handle the Tithe, let's take a look at who were the children of Israel, what are the Twelve Tribes of Israel, and who were the significant figures that would emerge from the tribes.

"Israel"

We will start with Abraham, the father of many nations, Genesis 17:1-4/Romans 4:16-17. God renamed him Abraham from Abram because of the faithfulness he had, even without a written law to follow. Now, Abraham had two sons, Ishmael whom he bore through his wife's handmaiden, Hager, and Isaac whom he bore through his wife, Sarah. God told Abraham that he will remember Ishmael, but his covenant was with Isaac and his seed for an everlasting covenant. Now, Isaac and his wife had twins, Esau and Jacob. When they were born, Esau came out first and Jacob followed by grabbing Esau's heel, which was a prophetic sign of the two brothers' future relationship, Genesis 25:26. Even in their mother's womb they fought, and God told Rebekah (Isaac's wife), Genesis 25:22,

> *And the children struggled together within her, and she said, if it be so, why am I thus? And she went to enquire of the LORD. And the LORD said unto her, two nations are in thy womb, and two manner of people shall be separated from thy bowels; and the one people shall be stronger than the other people and the elder shall serve the younger.*

When Esau and Jacob grew up, Isaac favored Esau more because of their similarities. When Isaac was old and felt as if he were close to death, he called Esau unto himself and told him to go out in the fields and bring him some meat to eat. Isaac's plan was to bless Esau before he died, by prophesying the blessings that God gave to Abraham. Rebekah heard of this and told Jacob to get some meat, and she would prepare it for his father. She told Jacob to go in with the meat and pretend that he was Esau in order to receive the blessings. Rebekah placed some of Esau's clothes on Jacob as well as some goat hair on his hands so that Jacob would smell and feel like his brother Esau whom was a very hairy man. This plan of theirs worked, and Jacob received the blessings, while Esau begged Isaac, his father, to bless him as well. Esau hated his brother, Jacob, for his deeds. The story goes on as Jacob was sent away by his father to find a wife. While he was gone he found a place to rest for the night and used a stone for his pillow. That night, Jacob had a dream of a ladder ascending into the heavens, with the angels of God descending and ascending on it. The Lord was standing above it, and he told Jacob he would be with him and would bring him back to this place, which Jacob named Bethel. (Later on we will see that this same location is where the city of Jerusalem and the Temple are erected.) Jacob awoke and said truly this is the place where God dwells and this is the gate to heaven. Jacob promised God that if he would keep him, he would give a tenth of everything the Lord blessed him with, Genesis 28:22. Now, Jacob met his uncle and stayed with him for a total of 14 years in order to earn his two wives, Leah and Rachel. From these two women, Jacob bore a total of 12 sons. When Jacob was returning to the land of his father, he sent messengers to his brother, Esau, so he would know if he was welcomed or not. The Bible said Jacob was afraid and fled with his two wives, maidservants, and 11 sons (at that time) across the brook of water. Jacob told his entire house to keep moving while he stayed there overnight alone. That night he wrestled with a man all night and would not let him go until he blessed him; for he knew this was not just a man. The man asked him what was his name, and when Jacob told him, the man changed his name to "Israel," Genesis 32:28. This is where the name Israel originated, and Jacob's (Israel's) 12 sons were the 12 tribes of Israel.

"Significant Figures from the 12 Tribes"

In Genesis 49 we see Israel (Jacob) much older now and close to death as he is blessing his 12 sons, the heads of the 12 tribes of Israel. Notice how he speaks prophetically to each of them, telling their past and future. He tells Simeon and Levi (Levi being the head of his tribe, the Levites),

> *I will divide them in Jacob and scatter them in Israel.*

This prophecy is two-fold as you will see later, when the two brothers defy their father and when God tells the people of Israel to not forget the Levite that is in your gates when he widens Israel's border (Deut 12:20). He then tells Judah,

> *Judah, thou art he whom thy brethren shall praise: thy hand shall be in the neck of thine enemies; thy father's children shall bow down before thee. Judah is a lion's whelp: from the prey, my son, thou art gone up: he stooped down, he couched as a lion, and as an old lion; who shall rouse him up? The sceptre shall not depart from Judah, nor a lawgiver from between his feet, until Shiloh come; and unto him shall the gathering of the people be. Binding his foal unto the vine, and his ass's colt unto the choice vine; he washed his garments in wine, and his clothes in the blood of grapes: His eyes shall be red with wine, and his teeth white with milk.*

So when Israel (Jacob) mentioned that Judah shall be praised, that he is a lion, and relating him to the choice vine, he was speaking a prophetic description of Jesus and how he would come out of the tribe of Judah (see Rev 5:5 and John 15:1-5). Not to get off the topic here, but praise be to God for this prophetic word about the Tribe of Judah. It is Judah in which our Lord Jesus genealogy came from by way of his earthly dad Joseph (Matthew 1:1-16)! Now, let's recap; at this point we see that Jacob was re-named "Israel," he had 12 sons which were the 12 tribes of himself, "Israel." His son, Levi, was the head of his tribe, the Levites, from which

Aaron and the Priests would emerge, and Judah was the tribe Jesus would come from.

"Levitical Priesthood"

So how did the Levitical priesthood begin and who ordained it? Let's begin with the birth of Levi to his father Jacob and his mother Leah. Levi was the third son born to Leah who was trying to win the love of Jacob by bearing him sons (Genesis 29:31-34). When Levi and his brothers were older, their sister, Dinah, was taken by the son of a Prince belonging to another tribe known as the Hi'-vites. The Prince's son lay with Dinah and defiled her. The Prince made a covenant with Jacob (Israel) that all of his males would circumcise themselves and become as one with Israel in order for Dinah to become the wife of the Prince's son. Jacob agreed to this, and it was done. Levi and his brother Simeon however, had other plans and they killed all of the males to include the Prince and his son (Genesis 34). Because of these two brothers combined treachery, Jacob (Israel) prophesied to them that they would no longer be united and that they would be divided in Jacob and scattered in Israel (Genesis 49:5-7). It is from this word, spoken over Levi, that the Tribe of Levite would not be numbered with the children of Israel and would not share the inheritance (Num 2:33/Deut 14:27).

Now, we all know the story of Moses and how he was born a slave but raised as a son of Pharaoh's daughter, but most people do not know that Moses was indeed born of the Tribe of Levi (Exodus 2:1-10). When God chose Moses to lead his people, (The Children of Israel), out of Egypt, God was establishing the Levitical Priesthood. This priesthood was responsible for guiding the Children of Israel (Jacob) in the commandments and ways of the living God! Aaron came into the picture because of Moses' insecurities concerning his ability to speak in front of people. God told

Moses to take his brother Aaron as his spokesman and that God would give Moses the words to give to Aaron (Exodus 4:10-17). After Moses and Aaron delivered the Children of Israel (Jacob) from the bondage of Egypt and into the wilderness of Mount Si'-nai, God began to establish his covenant and to give out his precise instructions! Outside of the "Ten Commandments," there were hundreds of things God commanded the Children of Israel to do. All of these different commandments combined to that which is known as "The Law of Moses." God established the Levites as the Priests to ensure these commandments were carried out in the proper manner.

Initially, Moses was led by God in the wilderness in the form of a thick cloud so that the people would see, hear, and believe Moses was chosen by God (Exodus 19:9/24:15). After this, God told Moses to take an offering from the people, who were willing to do so, of gold, silver, brass, and other items so that a sanctuary may be built and God would come down and dwell with them (Exodus 25-27). God knew Moses could not do everything, so he instructed him to bring his brother Aaron to him, and God would appoint him and his sons as the High Priest of the tabernacle (Leviticus 8). Now, Aaron and his sons had the responsibility of the vessels of the sanctuary and the altar, which was behind the veil. No one could enter this area except Aaron and his sons (Numbers 18:7-10). Outside of the veil was the responsibility of the remaining members of the Tribe of Levi that were of age (Numbers 3:6-13/8:1-26/18:2-4).

"The Camp Is Arranged"

Moses was instructed by God to number everyone according to their father's house. Remember, there were 12 Tribes represented here, which were the 12 Tribes of Israel (Jacob). The total number of people was 603,550. This did not include the Tribe of Levi, whom God told Moses not to include with the others. The Tribe of Levi was numbered separately, and their number came to 22,000 people. Now, Levi had three sons whom were Ger'-shon, Ko'-hath, and Me-ra'-ri. Each son's family of the Tribe of Levi had a specific position within the camp that encompassed the tabernacle (Numbers 3:6-39). Once the tabernacle was constructed exactly to God's instructions and dimensions, the cloud that once would only dwell with Moses descended on the tabernacle and it was known, from that day forward, as "The Tent of the Testimony" (Numbers 9:15).

As we discussed earlier, Aaron, his sons, and the priest from the Tribe of Levi had no part in the inheritance with the Children of Israel (Jacob). God told Aaron, he was their inheritance and in doing so would provide their substance (Numbers 18:20). Please remember this important key, as it will be crucial in understanding the Tithe.

"The People Murmur"

As the people continued in the commandments of God, they began to question God and his leadership. Several times the people would murmur against Moses and Aaron even accusing them of killing the people of God (Numbers 16:1-41). So God knew these people needed a sign that would prove to them who had been truly chosen of God!

> *And the LORD spake unto Moses, saying, Speak unto the children of Israel, and take of every one of them a rod according to the house of their fathers, of all their princes according to the house of their fathers twelve rods: write thou every man's name upon his rod. And thou shalt write Aaron's name upon the rod of Levi: for one rod shall be for the head of the house of their fathers. And thou shalt lay them up in the tabernacle of the*

God was tired of the murmurs coming from the children of Israel, even so for Moses sake. At one point God commanded Moses to bring Aaron and his wife Miriam into the tabernacle, and God cursed Miriam with leprosy for their murmurs (Numbers 12:5). So God told Moses to take a rod from the head of each tribe and place them in the Tabernacle, and whichever rod blossoms that tribe would be the chosen one of God to work in the tabernacle. This way God was saying since the Children of Israel wanted to complain about Moses and accuse him of not being the chosen one of God, he would show them by allowing their rods to stand as a witness to them of his choice. Each rod had the name of the head of their father's house written on it. God told Moses to place Aaron's name on the rod that represented the Tribe of Levi. Upon going into the tabernacle the next day, Moses found that Aaron's rod had flowers and blossoms on it. Therefore, God had chosen the Tribe of Levi to run the Tabernacle. This is how the Levitical Priesthood began.

As we follow the course of events with the Children of Israel, we see that in the book of Numbers, chapter 18, God is giving out his commandments to Aaron and the Levites on their purpose and responsibilities. Verse 1,

So the LORD said to Aaron, "You and your sons and your fathers' house (the house of Levi) with you shall bear iniquity in connection with the sanctuary; and you and your sons with you shall bear iniquity in connection with your priesthood. And with you bring your brethren also, the tribe of

Honestly, I could close right here, stop writing, and end this book with Amen. Notice what God said, *"I give your priesthood as a gift, and any one else who comes near shall be put to death"!* First of all, the tabernacle was a place where God said that he would meet the Children of Israel and to speak with them (Exodus 29:42). We know today that our bodies are the temple of God's spirit and not a structure built by hands (1 Corinthians 6:19). Secondly, the office of the priest is no longer that of only a certain tribe or sect of people, but is now that office belonging to Jesus Christ. Hebrews 9:11 reads, *"But Christ being come a High Priest of good things to come, by a greater and more perfect tabernacle, not made with hands, that is to say, not of this building; Neither by the blood of goats and calves, but by his own blood he entered in once into the holy place, having obtained eternal redemption for us."* So as you can see, the entire structure of the priesthood changed.

"The Order of the Tithe"

Now that we understand how the Levites became the caretakers of the tabernacle, we can continue in our quest to understanding the Tithe and its purpose. Let's get back to the establishment of the Tithe. In Numbers 18, verse 24 through 26, God said,

> *But the Tithes of the Children of Israel which they offer as an heave offering (a tenth of the tenth) unto the lord, I have given to the Levites to inherit: When ye take of the Children of Israel the tithes which I have given you from them for your inheritance, then ye shall offer up an heave offering of it for the lord, even a tenth part of the tithe.*

You see, God told the Children of Israel to give their tithe unto the Levites, because the Levites served in the Tabernacle of the Congregation to bear the iniquities of the Children of Israel. Therefore, out of the Children of Israel the Levites would have no inheritance. Now, out of the Tithe that was given to the Levites for their inheritance, the Levites were commanded of God to offer up a *Heave Offering* to the Lord. God called it, *A tenth of a tenth*; now, how many times have you heard this being taught in church? So what were the Levites supposed to do with this Tenth of a Tenth Heave Offering? God said in Numbers 18, verse 28,

> *Thus ye also shall offer an heave offering unto the LORD of all your tithes, which ye receive of the children of Israel; and ye shall*

give thereof the LORD'S heave offering to Aaron the priest. Out of all your gifts ye shall offer every heave offering of the LORD, of all the best thereof, even the hallowed part thereof out of it. Therefore thou shalt say unto them, When ye have heaved the best thereof from it, then it shall be counted unto the Levites as the increase of the threshing floor, and as the increase of the winepress. And ye shall eat it in every place, ye and your households: for it is your reward for your service in the tabernacle of the congregation. Eat it in every place, you and your entire family for it is your reward.

Let me make this perfectly clear. God does not need our money, food, wine, cattle, sheep or anything else we might think that we own. These provisions were established so that man could prove himself as loyal, honest, thankful and most of all obedient to the almighty God. That is why he told the Levites to consume this offering in his presence to show their gratitude. Now, I know this is somewhat new to most, considering for generations we have looked at the Tithe as money we pay to the local church. But this is the Word of God! Now, if it seems kind of hard to understand, read the entire 18th chapter, and then look at God's commandments in reverse order. You will then see that the Children of Israel paid the Tithes to the Levites; the Levites then took out of the Tithe the first and the best to give to Aaron for his portion of food and substance. Remember, Aaron and his sons were chosen by God to perform duties in the holy of holies at the altar. The Levites duties and responsibilities were in the Tabernacle of the Congregation. God gave the Tithe to the Levites for their food and substance, and out of that, he gave the best or the Heave Offering to Aaron. All of which was for their service as the High Priest and Priests of the Tabernacle.

"The Tithe as Part of the Sacrifices"

Most will find the above statement hard to swallow, but by reading Numbers 18:8-10 there is no doubt the sacrifices came from the Heave Offering. As we have discussed this Heave Offering not only came from the Tithe but it in itself was a form of Tithe. This is why God called it *"A Tenth of A Tenth"!* We see in verse 17 how the Tithe was part of the sacrifices of burnt offerings, but only the blood.

> *But the firstling of a cow, or the firstling of a sheep, or the firstling of a goat, you shall not redeem; they are holy. You shall sprinkle their blood upon the altar, and shall burn their fat as an offering by fire, a pleasing odor to the LORD; but their flesh shall be yours, as the breast that is waved and as the right thigh are yours. All the holy offerings which the people of Israel present to the LORD I give to you, and to your sons and daughters with you, as a perpetual due; it is a covenant of salt for ever before the LORD for you and for your offspring with you. And the LORD said to Aaron, "You shall have no inheritance in their land, neither shall you have any portion among them; I am your portion and your inheritance among the people of Israel."*

As we can plainly see, this practice of receiving the Tithe was God's way of providing for the Priests and for them to show God they are his people by giving thanks before him and receiving their reward from him. Now, I believe the practice of eating before the Lord originated with the establishment of "Israel." If we look again at Genesis 31:48, we can see the establishment of this offering known then as a *"Heap"* or pile of stones. Jacob had fled the land of his uncle, and taken his wives, Leah and Rachel, and all of their belongings. Rachel had stolen some of her father's idols and he pursued them. Laban (Jacob's mother's brother) and Jacob made a covenant at The Mount of Galeed, where they sacrificed and ate at the pillars and stones. A covenant was made for God to watch over them while they were apart so that both of them and their families would be taken care of and neither would cross over to the other's land to pursue the other. So now we can possibly see where this practice of eating the sacrifices before the Lord originated. Looking back to when Jacob first came in contact with his Uncle Laban, we can see how he was blessed and anointed by God to the point where his presence blessed Laban. Jacob was taking care of Laban's cattle and sheep when he decided that he too should be blessed by Laban since he was a blessing to him, Genesis 30:26-43. The story tells of how Jacob would place rods that gave an optical illusion to the animals of Laban and would cause them to conceive. Jacob would take the firstlings of all the cattle because they were maid speckled and spotted, and therefore not wanted of Laban. The Word of God said in verse 43,

> *And the man increased exceedingly, and had much cattle, and maidservants, and menservants, and camels, and Asses.*

God blessed "Israel" (Jacob) by allowing him to separate the flock and take most of them for himself as the mighty "Israel"! If it were not for these events Jacob would not have had the multitude of animals to provide substance for his family as well as for the purpose of providing sacrifices in the form of Tithing.

"Where to Bring the Tithes"

We continuously see God in Deuteronomy, the 12th chapter, laying the foundation of his commandments for the new land in which he was giving to the Children of Israel. In this passage of Scripture, God gives distinct orders of how the offerings, sacrifices and tithes are to be kept, or shall we say carried out. He said,

> *But unto the place which the Lord your God shall choose out of all your tribes (speaking of the 12 tribes of the Children of Israel) to put his name there, even for his dwelling shall ye seek, and thither thou shall bring your burnt offerings, your sacrifices, your TITHES and heave offerings of your land and your vows and your freewill offerings, and the firstlings of your herds and of your flocks: and there ye shall eat before the lord your God and ye shall rejoice in all that ye put your hand unto, ye and your house holds, wherein the lord thy God hath blessed thee.* Verse 32 reads, *What thing soever I command you, observe to do it: thou shalt not add thereto, nor diminish from it.*

Now again, how much more clearly does God have to be in his direction? He told the Children of Israel to take the Tithe, which again was cattle, sheep, or the money made in selling them, to the place where he has placed his name, and do not add nor take away from what he said. An example of adding to this commandment might be telling people that your church or building is the place to bring the Tithe. You see, somehow the Body of Christ has mistaken what God had established as a celebration before him for a systematic ritual that we must do in order to keep the finances flowing for bill consumption in our churches. I don't want to get too far ahead of myself, but this old covenant that God had with his people changed, and with that change came a new way of conducting ourselves in every aspect of our service, dedication, and obedience to God. Just look at the New Testament and its obvious changes from the old way of doing things.

The book of Hebrews talks about a much-needed change. Hebrews 7:12,

> *For the priesthood being changed, there is made of necessity a change also of the law.*

This change in the law consisted of the entire formula that God gave to the Children of Israel in order for them to receive their righteousness. Now, don't focus too much on Melchizedek that is mentioned in the book of Hebrews, because we will discuss him later on. Let us continue in the Tithes history. In Deuteronomy, the 14th chapter, verses 22 through 29, we see God giving yet another part of his commandments concerning the Tithe, he said,

> *Thou shalt truly tithe all the increase of thy seed that the field bringeth forth year by year. and thou shalt eat before the lord thy God, in the place which HE SHALL CHOOSE to place his name there.* Verse 24 reads, *And if the journey be too far from thee, then shalt thou exchange it for money, and bind up the money in thine hand, and shalt go unto the place which the lord thy God shall choose: And thou shalt spend that money for whatsoever your heart desires, for oxen, or for sheep, or for wine, or for strong drink or for whatsoever thy soul desireth: And thou shalt eat there before the lord thy God.*

God simply wanted the Children of Israel to be thankful for what he had done for them throughout the year. Also by bringing the tithe of everything before God and using it in his presence was just another way of saying, here Lord, this is the tenth and the best of what you have done for me. God didn't want it to go to waste, so he instructed them to eat thereof in the place that he had chosen. The money that was received as a trade for the goods was also spent before the Lord in that place for whatever their hearts desired, but there was also something else God wanted them to do with it. In verses 27 through 29, God said,

> *And the Levite that is within thy gates; thou shalt not neglect him; for he hath no part nor inheritance with thee.*

Not only did God say to remember the Levite, in verse 28 and 29 God said to remember the stranger, the fatherless, and the widow, which are within thy gates. God said,

> *If ye do this he would bless thee in all the work of thine hand.*

This practice was to be done at the end of every three years. I wonder how many churches that do enforce the commandment of the LAW to tithe, are using it for the people mentioned here. I am sure that most churches either donate money or have a program established for the needy, but the majority of their Tithe usage is for paying the debts of the church, including the staff that is on the payroll. If we are to Tithe and are then following this practice of paying bills with it, we would not be doing it according to God's word. I will take it even further by saying it was not the priest's responsibility to help those in need but that of the Children of Israel! Remember, God is not speaking to the priest (the Levites); he is speaking to the Children of Israel as evident in verse 22,

> *Thou shalt truly tithe all the increase of thy seed, that the field bringeth forth year by year,* and verse 27, *And the Levite that is within thy gates; thou shalt not forsake him; for he hath no part nor inheritance with the.*

Nevertheless, this was God's plan to bless the Children of Israel through their obedience in the commandment of tithe. As you can see, this process of taking the tithe, using it in the place where God established his name, and helping the less fortunate around them was a continuous cycle of blessings for all as long as the Children of Israel would continue to be obedient. Now ask yourself, does my church practice the Tithe in accordance with the Scripture that I just read? The answer to this question 99.9% of the time is No! Now, the only thing that is not known at this point is the location of the place (the storehouse) where God said he would choose out of all of the tribes of Israel to put his name there for the Tithe to be brought? We find the answer to this question in 2nd Chronicles, chapter 6, verse 6, where God said,

> *But I have chosen Jerusalem that my name might be there; and have chosen David to be over my people Israel.*

If we are to truly tithe according to the word of God, we should all be sending, or better yet taking, our tithes across the sea to Jerusalem to eat thereof or spend the money that we traded our blessings for in that place where God said he has chosen to place his name, "Jerusalem!" Not First Baptist, or the Assemblies of God, nor Saint Francis of Assisi church, but Jerusalem. Some may say, "Well, the place where his name is could be any church establishment, but as you can plainly see, that is not what God said in his word." Remember, he said *"And if the Journey be too far"*! Our local churches are not too far away from us, besides that would mean that any person could just open a church, and automatically that place is where God has placed his name; I don't think so! We all know that every place that is called the House of the Lord is not always holding true to its title. God's word is true, and he has already said where the storehouse is and that place was Jerusalem! God even warned them to not take the Tithe somewhere else and eat of it, Deuteronomy 12:17,

> *Thou mayest not eat within thy gates the tithe of thy corn, or of thy wine, or of thy oil, or the firstlings of thy herds or of thy flock, nor any of thy vows which thou vowest, nor thy freewill*

offerings, or heave offering of thine hand: But thou must eat them before the LORD thy God in the place which the LORD thy God shall choose, thou, and thy son, and thy daughter, and thy manservant, and thy maidservant, and the Levite that is within thy gates: and thou shalt rejoice before the LORD thy God in all that thou puttest thine hands unto. Take heed to thyself that thou forsake not the Levite as long as thou livest upon the earth. When the LORD thy God shall enlarge thy border, as he hath promised thee, and thou shalt say, I will eat flesh, because thy soul longeth to eat flesh; thou mayest eat flesh, whatsoever thy soul lusteth after. If the place which the LORD thy God hath chosen to put his name there be too far from thee, then thou shalt kill of thy herd and of thy flock, which the LORD hath given thee, as I have commanded thee, and thou shalt eat in thy gates whatsoever thy soul lusteth after. Even as the roebuck and the hart is eaten, so thou shalt eat them: the unclean and the clean shall eat of them alike. Only be sure that thou eat not the blood. Verse 26, Only thy holy things which thou hast, and thy vows, thou shalt take, and go unto the place which the LORD shall choose: ²⁷ And thou shalt offer thy burnt offerings, the flesh and the blood, upon the altar of the LORD thy God: and the blood of thy sacrifices shall be poured out upon the altar of the LORD thy God, and thou shalt eat the flesh. ²⁸ Observe and hear all these words which I command thee, that it may go well with thee, and with thy children after thee for ever, when thou doest that which is good and right in the sight of the LORD thy God.

How much clearer should God be in order for us to understand? Let's go a little deeper in our discussion of the place where God said he would place his name. In 2 Chronicles, 33:7, we see God being even more specific of his storehouse that is in Jerusalem,

> *God had said to David and to Solomon his son, "In this house, and in Jerusalem, which I have chosen before all the tribes of Israel, will I put my name for ever."*

So as you can see, God gave specific instructions for the Children of Israel to bring their Tithes, regardless of how far they were, to Jerusalem where his name would be over his house forever! God also instructed them that if the journey is too far, that they could eat flesh within their gates but they still had to bring those holy things to that place and to not forget about the Levite within their gates. God said for them to do this forever! So that pretty much kills the idea of a building somewhere else in the world as being a place to bring the Tithe!

"The Temple"

The house that God was talking about was the Temple that David wanted to build and his son, Solomon, later did build (1 Chronicles 28:2-6). To give a quick preview, David was anointed at an early age. He slew the Palestine warrior, Goliath, and became well known throughout the land. God sent Samual the prophet and chose David as the next king of Israel. David is a descendent of the Tribe of Judah. His son, King Solomon, built the temple, and it was destroyed under his watch as well. The Temple was a replica of the Tent of the Testimony that Moses was commanded by God to make. The temple had all of the features of the tent as well as others, but this was the permanent location for the Tent of the Testimony and all of its components to include the presence of God (1 Kings 5/6/7:13-51/8:1-21).

The temple was built and destroyed several times and witnessed by the Levites who were still shown as the caretakers of the house of God, as seen in Ezra 3:12. The destruction came mostly due to the placement of unclean items in it and the absence of the Ark of the Covenant, which gave God's enemies the ability to destroy the temple due to God's presence not being there. This cycle of destroying and rebuilding the Temple would continuously happen throughout the Old Testament, the New, and beyond, because of the hearts of man allowing such things to enter into the house of God. God said in Hosea 9:15,

> *All their wickedness is in Gilgal: for there I*
> *hated them: for the wickedness of their doings*
> *I will drive them out of mine **house**, I will love*
> *them no more: all their princes are revolters.*

Jesus himself predicted the destruction of the temple, in Luke 21:5,

> *And as some spake of the temple, how it was*
> *adorned with goodly stones and gifts, he said,*
> *As for these things which ye behold, the days*
> *will come, in the which there shall not be left*
> *one stone upon another, that shall not be*
> *thrown down.*

This prophecy that Jesus was speaking of would be the final destruction of the temple, until the attempt of the Anti-Christ to rebuild it; that is written in Daniel 11:31. The Temple, in Jerusalem, was and is to this day, the location that God instructed his people to bring the Tithe forever.

So far we have examined how the Tithe was an inheritance for the Levites, how God commanded them to give a "Heave Offering" from the Tithe called "A Tenth of a Tenth" to Aaron for his inheritance, and how out of the Heave Offering Aaron and his sons would offer up the blood from the best animals as the sacrifices, but the meat they would eat before God. God told them to eat this offering in the place where he placed his name, "Jerusalem," and the house that God was referring to was the temple that King Solomon built.

Now, let's take a look at the location within the temple known as "The Storehouse" in which all of the tithes, offerings, and sacrifices were kept. This "Storehouse" was located in the place where God's name rested, Jerusalem! In the book of Nehemiah, chapter 10, verse 38, through chapter 14, we see how God had certain people from the 12 tribes of the Children of Israel to dwell in Jerusalem and to be the keepers/overseers of the storehouses.

Have you ever wondered why there is a gigantic wall around the city where God has placed his name? Could its purpose have anything to do with all of the attacks throughout history on this holy place? Besides the constant battle for the land in this area, what do you think the thieves were after? Do you think that just maybe, after years and years of this continuous cycle of blessings, it could have created an abundance of goods?

According to the WORD OF GOD, the wall of Jerusalem was dedicated in a ceremonial-type celebration where not only did they rejoice but there were also appointments of certain guard post. This is clearly stated in the 12th and 13th chapters of Nehemiah; verse 27 reads,

> *And at the dedication of the wall of Jerusalem they sought the Levites out of all their places, to bring them to Jerusalem, to keep the dedication with gladness, both with thanksgiving and with singing with cymbals, stringed instruments and with harps.* Verse 31 reads, *Then I brought up the princes of Judah upon the wall, and appointed two great companies of them that gave thanks, whereof one went on the right hand upon the wall toward the dung gate.* Verse 38 reads, *And the*

other company of them that gave thanks went over against them, and I after them, and the half of the people upon the wall, from beyond the tower of the furnaces even unto the broad wall. Verse 44 reads, *And at that time were some appointed over the chambers for the treasures, for the offerings, for the first fruits, and for the tithes, to gather into them out of the fields of the cities the portions of the LAW for the priests and Levites.*

Notice how some were appointed over the different chambers to receive from the people. The term "Portions of the Law" referred to the offerings, first fruits, and the Tithe that was commanded of the Children of Israel to give to the priests. The reason for separating these items into chambers simply made it easier to watch over them and even to prepare them for their individual purposes. Remember the priests had to take out of the Tithe in order to have the Heave offering. Verse 1 of chapter 13 talks about how there were individuals that were not allowed within the congregation.

On that day they read in the Book of Moses (The LAW) in the audience of the people; and therein was found written that the Am'-mon-ite and the Mo'-ab-ite should not come into the congregation of God for ever.

This is why the wall was built; in order to keep those that did not have any inheritance out and to stop those that would come into the city to steal the goods. In the 39th verse of chapter 10, we see a commandment to not forsake the House of our God; being New Testament believers, we now know that the House/Temple of our God is our body.

In 2 Corinthians, chapter 6, verse 16, Paul said,

And what agreement hath the temple of God with idols? For ye are the Temple of the living God.

There is no longer a need to have a certain place where a priest would go to offer up sacrifices unto God, for we ourselves should be a living sacrifice, meaning that every day of our lives we are to take up our cross and follow Christ! We ourselves are now the *"Temple of God"*! Just as the priest would offer up sacrifices in the temple, we are also to offer up sacrifices, but not as those of old.

> *For the bodies of those beasts, whose blood is brought into the sanctuary by the high priest for sin, are burned outside the camp. Wherefore Jesus also, that he might set apart the people with his own blood, suffered outside the gate. Let us go forth therefore unto him outside the camp, bearing his reproach.* Verse 15, *By him therefore let us offer the sacrifice of praise to God continually, that is, the fruit of our lips giving thanks to his name.*   Hebrews 13:10-15

In John, chapter 2, verse 19, Jesus said,

> *Destroy this Temple, and in three days I will raise it up.*

The people did not understand him and thought that he was talking about the building in which they came to worship, but he was talking about his body. Earlier in this same passage of Scripture, we see that Jesus went up to Jerusalem and found people selling and trading in the Temple of God. Going back to the origin of the city, we see why they were doing this. It was because of the Commandment given by God to Tithe that they were there bringing their money into the location were God said he would choose to place his name. So why didn't Jesus just smile and say, "Ahh, the people are doing just as they were told." No! He said, *"My house shall be called for all nations the house of prayer, but ye have made it a Den of Thieves."* If the Holy Spirit is ministering to you right now, like I know he is, you will see that Jesus is showing us that we as the new Temple of God should also be the

House of prayer and praise. Jesus was prophesying, at that time, about the change in temple worship.

Getting back to the message at hand, the Children of Israel had taken the things that God had established, such as bringing the Tithe to Jerusalem, and corrupted it by moving there selling and trading into the very Temple and not just leaving it out in the city itself. It was the Priest (Levites) who was to actually be in the Temple, and Jesus knew this. Not only did he know of the disobedience but also of the trickery and lies and stealing involved in the buying and trading. We can see this best in John 2:13.

> *And the Jews' Passover was at hand, and Jesus went up to Jerusalem, and found in the temple those that sold oxen and sheep and doves, and the changers of money sitting: and when he had made a whip of small cords, he drove them all out of the temple, and the sheep, and the oxen; and poured out the changers' money, and overturned the tables; and said unto them that sold doves, Take these things hence; make not my Father's house a house of merchandise.*

Again, the people were doing what their father's fathers had done for years that stemmed from the Commandment to Tithe, but Jesus was bringing forth the very manifestation of the change in the entire priesthood that had been prophesied from days of old.

> *Behold the days are coming, says the LORD, when I will make a new covenant with the house of Israel and the house of Judah, not like the covenant which I made with their fathers.* Jeremiah 31:31

"The Tithe's Original vs. Present Purpose"

If the ordinances of old were still in effect it would be detrimental to the Body of Christ.   In 1st Corinthians, chapter 12, verse 13, Paul said,

> *For by one spirit are we all baptized into one*
> *body, whether we be Jews or gentiles, bond or*
> *free.*

I believe that pretty well covers everyone. Considering all nationalities of people can receive salvation and all of God's promises are given to them that do, bringing the tithes and offerings into the storehouse, as practiced in the days of old, would not apply now due to it only applying to a select few back then. We know God told them to practice this in the place where he chose his name and that place was Jerusalem.   This command was given to the Children of Israel and their priest the Levites, so it would not apply to us in the same form of a commandment. You say, "Well, we are God's people now and that is why we Tithe." Well, God said, *"Whatever the law says, it speaks to those who are under the law"* (see Romans 3:19).

So you could follow this method of "Tithing" as a formula to give by using the ten percent rule, but you would not attempt to return to those practices that involved the blood sacrifices; would you? Well, by trying to follow the Tithe according to how God established it, you would be required to! You say we do not need the blood sacrifices of animals anymore because they were for the remissions of sin, and you would be correct in saying so! Jesus Christ's once and final sacrifice of himself is how Christians (or followers of Christ) are to receive our salvation. It is also through his various teachings that we learn obedience in by which we will receive our blessings. The Tithe was used by God to teach the Children of Israel obedience. At the same time God gave the Tithe to the Levites and the Heave Offering out of the Tithe to Aaron, for their inheritance as the Priest/High Priest of the Tabernacle. Aaron used the blood from his portion of the Tithe (Heave Offering) to offer it as a sacrifice for sin (see Numbers 18:8-32). So if the sacrifices were fulfilled/done away with by Jesus, then would not the source for the sacrifices also be done away with as well? The requirement, to give the Tithe to a priesthood that served in a tabernacle made of hands, has been fulfilled through Christ. It is only through Christ that we can receive anything from God.

"Where Are the Levites?"

If the requirement of giving the Tithe to Aaron and the Levites never changed, then we (Christians of today) would have to trace the genealogy of Aaron and the Levites to find their living descendants. Once we found them, we would have to pay our Tithes to them because God said,

> *This is a lasting ordinance for the generations to come.* Numbers 18:23

Let's take a look at Hebrews 9:1-6 and 8; Verse 1 says,

> *Then verily the first covenant had also ordinances of divine service, and a earthly sanctuary. For there was a tabernacle made; the first, wherein was the candlestick, and the table, and the shewbread; which is called the sanctuary and after the second veil, the tabernacle which is called the holiest of all, verse 6, Now when these things were thus ordained, the priests went always into the first tabernacle, accomplishing the service of God. But into the second went the high priest alone once every year, not without blood which he offered for himself, and for the people.*

Now notice what point it makes in this next verse, verse 8,

> *The holy Ghost this signifying that the way into the holiest of all was not yet made manifest, while as the first tabernacle was yet standing: which was symbolic, in which were offered both gifts and sacrifices, that could not make him that did the service perfect.*

The tabernacle is said to be symbolic in this passage of Scripture, representing Christ.

Verse 11 reads,

> *But Christ being come an high priest of good things to come by a greater and more perfect tabernacle, not made with hands.*

You see, Christ is our High Priest who sits at the right hand of the Father for us, just as Moses and Aaron, the High Priest of old, would go into the holy place. So again, if there is no longer a need for the offerings and blood sacrifices, which were commandments of the LAW, why would there be a need for the tithes that were also a God-given commandment, written under the LAW, that provided the substance for the sacrifices? (Numbers 18:9-10) I will tell you why, people will come up with every reason in the book to justify the practice of Tithing, but the truth of the matter is the Tithe was clearly a practice for the Children of Israel and their Priests!

Jesus is our priest, and he does not need a source of food from us that is in the form of animals to make sacrifices unto God! Jesus was and is the living Sacrifice, so give him the sacrifice of praise!

"Malachi"

At this point, we are coming to the end of the history of the tithe. The last thing that we will examine, concerning the Tithe, is the book of Malachi. Let's start with the section that is overlooked the most—ALL OF THE BOOK OF MALACHI! The interesting thing about Malachi is that the word of God that came forth was mostly for the Priest! Oh my, did I say that? No, I did not say it; I repeated it from the Word of God. Malachi 2:4 reads,

> *And ye shall know that I have sent this commandment unto you, that my covenant might be with Levi, saith the LORD of hosts. My covenant was with him of life and peace; and I gave them to him for the fear wherewith he feared me, and was afraid before my name. The law of truth was in his mouth, and iniquity was not found in his lips: he walked with me in peace and equity, and did turn many away from iniquity. For the priest's lips should keep knowledge, and they should seek the law at his mouth: for he is the messenger of the LORD of hosts. But ye are departed out of the way; ye have caused many to stumble at the law; ye have corrupted the covenant of Levi, saith the LORD of hosts. Therefore have I also made you contemptible and base before all the people, according as ye have not kept my ways, but have been partial in the law.*

Partial in the LAW—now that is an interesting statement. What does God mean, *"ye have not kept my ways, but have been partial in the law"?* God is talking about all of his instructions that were given, not specifically to Levi, but to the Tribe of Levi to pass down for all of their descendents to observe. The Tribe of Levi was the priest, and it was their responsibility to live according to the Law and to ensure that the Children of Israel did the same. That is why God said,

> *Ye have caused many to stumble at the law;*
> *ye have corrupted the covenant of Levi.*

The *Covenant of Levi* was not directly with Levi himself, but with his Tribe. When God would speak of Levi, he was talking about those from the entire tribe that were to be the Priests. Although the prophetic word spoken over Levi by his father Jacob came to pass, the prophecy did not specifically note a priesthood in Levi. It did, however, state that Simeon and Levi would be divided in Jacob and scattered in Israel (Genesis 49:7). This simply meant that when God extended Israel's borders, each tribe would have their own land except for Levi's.

God did, however, command Moses to instruct the Children of Israel to give cities and suburbs, out of their possessions, to the Levites to live in (Num 35:1-5/Joshua 21:1-2). God knew that he would use the Tribe of Levi as the priest and that they would not have an inheritance or land to possess as their own. The only inheritance for the Priest would be the sacrifices, which were in the form of the Tithe (Joshua 14/Num 18:21). We all know that God's thoughts are not our thoughts and that we prophesy in part, so these reasons could be the answer to why the Levitical Priesthood was not mentioned in the prophecy spoken by Jacob (Israel). The actual *Covenant of Peace* mentioned in the above passage of Scripture from Malachi, did not happen in Levi's lifetime. This covenant that God made was with the Tribe of Levi by way of Aaron's grandson, Phin'-e-has. (Num 25:10)

So in Malachi 2:4, God was telling the priest that the people were falling short of or misinterpreting the law because of their substandard teachings. God told the priest that *"Ye have corrupted the covenant of Levi"* because part of his covenant with the Tribe of Levi was placing the Children of Israel under the leadership of the priest. This is evident even in the verses of Malachi 2:4, when he said, *"And I gave them to him for the fear wherewith he feared me"*. God entrusted the priest with the Children of Israel because they feared God and would therefore obey his commandments and teach them as well. The priest that Malachi was speaking to, however, had corrupted this covenant that God originally made with their father's fathers in the Tribe of Levi.

God was telling the priest that they were responsible for causing many to stumble at the Law because of their lack of leadership and instruction. This lack of attention by the priest caused the people to begin their own Traditions of Men in the acceptance of idols to be placed within the temple.

In this last segment we are going to discuss the most widely quoted Scripture concerning the tithe, Malachi 3:7-10, *"Will a man rob God?"* Now, I am sure that most people can quote this Scripture word for word, but again, God was directing the majority of his conviction to the priest. People get so hooked on this one Scripture that they don't even pay any attention to the chapters and verses before it. In chapter 1, God is rebuking the priest for bringing lame and sick sacrifices. God asked the priest, in verse 13, *"Should I accept this of your hand?"* Think about it; God was not talking to the people because it was the Priest that was given the Commandment to receive the Tithe. God specifically commanded the Levites to not do this in Leviticus 22:20. In chapter 2 we see God again rebuking the Priests for,

> *Departing out of the way; ye have caused many to stumble at the law.*

God convicted the Priests for corrupting the covenant he made with the Tribe of Levi which can be referenced to the Levitical Priesthood in Exodus 29:9/40:15, and Numbers 25:10. In chapter 2:10, the people are practicing idolatry, and in verse 14, they are divorcing their spouse for selfish and wrongful reasons. So why is the tithe the only sin that is pointed out when Malachi is mentioned? I will tell you why; people use this Scripture to justify tithing because of the added threat of a curse. In verse 6, God is giving out his order to the sons of Jacob about the tithe. As we previously discussed, the lineage of Abraham who paid tithes to Melchizedek, was Jacob renamed Israel. From Jacob, the 12 Tribes of Israel were Jacob's 12 sons. Levi was the son of Jacob that was given the office of the Priesthood. Now, this is why we see the prophet Malachi speaking to all of the descendants of Abraham or *Sons of Jacob*, which included the people as well as the Priests. In verse 7, notice what God is saying to the people and the priest.

> *Even from the Days of your fathers ye are gone away from mine ordinances, and have not kept them.*

What is he speaking of? The phrase *"days of your fathers"* is plural here meaning generations of fathers. In the next few lines, he said, *"ye are gone away from mine ordinances and have not kept them"*. The word ordinances mean a group of authoritative rules or LAWS; God was talking about "ALL" the commandments of the LAW that was mentioned by the prophet thus far; not just the Tithe. None of these commandments had been carried out like God had instructed. This is why in verse 7, God said,

> *Return unto me, and I will return unto you.*

The only way for the Children of Israel and the priest to return unto God would be to start obeying "ALL" of his many Laws from the book of Moses. Throughout the generations up to this particular point in time that Malachi was speaking, the people were indeed not Tithing according to God's commandment, but again they were not doing any of the other things that we discussed. So the Children of Israel and the priest needed to know what they should do or where could they begin their journey back to God's love, will, and protection. This is why Malachi spoke a word of knowledge that the people were thinking and asking themselves, when he said, *But ye said, wherein shall we return?* Malachi's answer was for them to start with being obedient to the commandment that instructed the Children of Israel to give the Tithe to the Levites for their inheritance.

"The Importance of the Tithe"

Understand that without the Tithe, the Levites would have no inheritance, which would mean they could not perform their duties in the temple. Therefore, the Priest would have to now work for their food in the fields. This means no priest to offer sacrifices for the sins of the people, which was God's very plan for their atonement during that time. One could see how detrimental this falling away from God's commandments would be; not just due to disobedience, but it would cause a halt to the entire process in which God established so he could be their God!

This was not the first time in history where the priest went away from God's Ordinances. In Nehemiah 13:10, we see the Priests of that particular time had done the same thing. They stopped receiving the Tithe and returned to their fields to work. This was not their purpose in life, for God's commandment to receive the Tithe was his way of providing food and substance for Aaron and the Levites (Priest). The Levites were not to work in the fields but in the house of God. They would receive the Tithe to live off of for food. This happened well before the prophet Malachi's day (Joshua 13:14,33/18:7/Num 18:7,21). In addition, God was reminding the Levites that his call on their life, as the priest for the Children of Israel, had not changed (read Romans 11:29). The priest had to return unto God by receiving the Tithe and giving the offerings from it for themselves as well as the Children of Israel. Remember, the priest took the Tithe for themselves, gave out of the Tithe the Heave Offering to Aaron and his sons, and they had to offer the blood and eat the flesh there at the altar. That is why Malachi quoted God in verse 10, by saying,

> *Bring ye all the tithes into the storehouse, that there may be meat (or food) in mine house.*

So again at the end of verse 7, God told the Children of Israel to return unto him and he would return unto them. He was not just talking about the tithe but all of the different areas of the LAW that were being forsaken. Malachi said unto them,

> *But ye said wherein shall we return? Will a man rob God? Yet ye have robbed me. But ye say wherein have we robbed thee? In tithes and offerings.*

This particular ordinance or statute of the LAW was indeed the commandment to tithe that God gave to Moses, and Moses gave it to the Children of Israel! In verse 9, God told the people,

> *Ye are cursed with a curse for ye have robbed me.*

This was their punishment for their disobedience to God's LAW. Again, he is still speaking of the commandment to tithe. The same Tithe God gave to the Levites for their inheritance as a source of food. I will point out to you again in verse 10, God said, *Bring ye all the Tithes into the storehouse that there may be **Meat** in my house."* Understand that God was reminding both the Children of Israel and the priest that without the Tithe there would not be any meat/blood for the offerings and food for the priest to eat. The simple fact is the people had robbed God in tithes and offerings because they stopped bringing the Tithe to the Levites, which in turn did not have blood to offer or meat to eat unto God. This is the reason for the priest returning to the field to work for their substance. So the Children of Israel were not practicing several commandments of the law as mentioned earlier. God wanted them to return to the ordinances established in the book of Moses (The LAW). He was not just simply telling them to Tithe, but to return to practicing ALL OF THE LAW!

"The Curse"

The curse that was initiated here because of their disobedience was the same curse that Moses spoke of when he said,

> *But it shall come to pass, if thou wilt not hearken unto the voice of the Lord thy God, to observe to do ALL OF HIS COMMANDMENTS AND HIS STATUTES which I command thee this day; that ALL THESE CURSES shall come upon thee, and overtake thee. (Deut 28:15)*

I believe it is so very important for the Body of Christ to understand the passage of Scripture in Malachi and how it references the curse under the Law of Moses! Later, in chapter two "What is the Law", we will conduct an intensive comparison of the curse spoken in the book of Malachi vs. the proclaimed curses by Moses at mount E'-bal. The book of Malachi does not accurately describe the state of the Body of Christ when it is used out of context to denote a curse. This curse was indeed spoken over the Children of Israel and should not be used in the same manner over the Body of Christ. Not only is it used to show the church of today how serious God was about the tithe, but it is almost as though it is used as a threat or scare tactic that just hovers above everyone's head in order to secure money in the form of the Tithe. But you say, "What about the promise of the windows of heaven being opened to those that obey?" Well, this is promising, but as we have already seen, and will see this method of receiving God's blessing was only for a select few, which were under the Law. As Paul said in Galatians 4:21,

*Tell me, you who desire to be under law, do
you not hear the law?*

Some may say yes, this was for God's people, the Children of Israel, but we are now his children, so it applies to us as well. I say unto you, nay! The tithe was strictly an ordinance under the first covenant (The LAW). Again, I speak in the words of Paul in Romans 3:19,

*Now we know that whatever the law says it
speaks to those who are under the law.*

The Children of Israel were commanded, *Under The Law,* to give the Tithe as an inheritance to the Levites. We have a new covenant with God through our Lord Jesus Christ. The Children of Israel, along with the Levites, received their blessings by not just obeying the Law of the tithe, but by the other acts required for righteousness, which was under the LAW as well (Deut 6:25). We as the Body of Christ shall receive our blessings and righteousness by following Christ and his many lessons, lifestyle, parables, and teachings of GIVING, which is under Grace!

"How Could We Be Missing It?"

Remember now, we are talking about the religious leaders of the Bible, who would drift away from the truth in God's word. In the Old Testament, it was the priest, and in the New Testament, it was the Pharisees and Scribes. So my point is that today, our religious leaders are no different in that they have the ability to misunderstand the word of God! If the priest of Old and the Scribes and Pharisees of New missed it, what makes the leadership of today believe they are beyond making mistakes? Before we move on, let me point out another obvious example of how we are missing it when it comes to the tithe. Moses was chosen by God to deliver his people from the bondage of Egypt. Moses told God that he had a speech impediment, so God told him to take his brother Aaron the Levite (Exodus 4:10). Now, if Aaron were a Levite, then that would make Moses one as well considering they were brothers (Num 26:59). This would explain why God chose Moses and Aaron; it was because of his covenant with the House of Levi.

When God gave out his commandments, statutes and judgments on the two mountains (Ger'-i-zim and E'-bal), he told the people they had to observe and to do all his commandments, or they would be cursed. This is where the curse in Malachi comes from. Now, if you look in Deuteronomy chapter 12 through chapter 26, you can see some of the statutes that God gave out along with that of the tithe. This is where I will make my point of how we are missing it. Chapter 26 lists the tithe and how we are to carry it out. Even though most of these instructions are not carried out today as they were then, most would still agree with the overall concept of the tithe that is listed. But if you will, just turn back a couple of pages and look at chapter 21:18, you will see another commandment that the Children of Israel were required to follow. This statute, concerning the way that God instructs the Children of Israel to handle a rebellious son, reads,

> *If a man have a stubborn and rebellious son, which will not obey the voice of his father, or the voice of his mother, and that, when they have chastened him, will not hearken unto them: Then shall his father and his mother lay hold on him, and bring him out unto the elders of his city and unto the gate of his place; And they shall say unto the elders of his city, this our son is stubborn and rebellious, he will not obey our voice; he is a glutton, and a drunkard. And all the men of his city shall stone him with stones, that he die.*

Now, if we are to continue with the practice of Tithing that is listed in chapter 26, are we to adhere to the Law of the Rebellious Son as well? For those that proclaim the tithe as a practice of today and cursing people who do not Tithe, they are literally telling the Body of Christ to revert back to the days of stoning as well! It is all the Word of God—is it not? That is what most pastors will say when confronted with the question, "Is the tithe still for today?" So what distinguishes one Law of the Old Covenant from another Law of the Old Covenant? Nothing—that's what! Again, the Children of Israel had to obey all of the Law and not just the ones that they agreed with or benefited from (Deuteronomy 6:25/27:9-10).

"The Traditions of Men"

As with our discussion of the temple and how by the bringing in of idols it was constantly being corrupted, it was indeed the fault of the priest for this blasphemy. I dare to speculate that along with these idols came a distinct change or moving away from the specific commandments of God. This is how the Traditions of Men managed to infiltrate the ministry by starting traditions at some point after the actions of a man instead of what God has commanded. In Mark 7:5 we see Jesus dealing with a prime example of the Traditions of Men.

> *Then the Pharisees and scribes asked him, why walk not thy disciples according to the tradition of the elders, but eat bread with unwashen hands? He answered and said unto them, well hath Esaias prophesied of you hypocrites, as it is written, this people honoureth me with their lips, but their heart is far from me. Howbeit in vain do they worship me, teaching for doctrines the commandments of men. For laying aside the commandment*

of God, ye hold the tradition of men, as the washing of pots and cups: and many other such like things ye do. And he said unto them, Full well ye reject the commandment of God, that ye may keep your own tradition.

Jesus was pointing out here how the Pharisees and Scribes were attempting to condemn him for eating without washing their hands as if it were a sin. A sin that was created in the minds of man made to override the commandments of God. Jesus answered them with a word of truth by saying,

Are ye so without understanding also? Do ye not perceive, that whatsoever thing from without (or outside) entereth into the man, it cannot defile him; Because it entereth not into his heart, but into the belly, and goeth out into the draught (or is eliminated) purging all meats (or purifying all foods)?

Jesus was showing them how they have taken the commandments of God and foolishly changed them into something that they could use to justify their own ideology. This word from our Lord is also a good example of how the things of old were fulfilled and changed by our Savior, in that under the Law, there were certain foods that would defile a person. Here Jesus was giving the fulfillment of that Law. He is God's word in the flesh, is he not?

Jesus gave another example of how the religious leaders of his time had taken the Law and corrupted it when he said,

*Woe unto you, Scribes and Pharisees, hypocrites! For ye pay **tithe** of mint and anise and cumin, and have omitted the weightier matters of the law, judgment, mercy, and faith: these ought ye to have done, and not to leave the other undone. Matthew 23:23*

Jesus called them "Hypocrites" for paying Tithes, which were part of the law, and not doing the other parts. So let me ask you a question, if we are to Tithe and we are not doing the other parts of the law, are we not hypocrites as well? Have we started a Tradition of Men by using the commandment to Tithe that was under the Old Covenant, and placing it in the New Covenant? Please beloved, do not think it strange, because if you look hard enough around your own circle of the Body of Christ, I am sure you can find quite a few traditions that have nothing to do with the Word of God! Let me help you out; good examples of this deception that are found in the traditions of men are Christmas and Easter.

Now, I will not go into the discussion of when these events represented here actually happened, but I will say this, the Bible says that when Jesus was born, the angel of the Lord appeared unto the shepherds that were tending the flocks in the field (Luke 2:8). Well, it has been noted that during the month of December, there are no shepherds in the field because of the weather. Trust me, I served my country in the desert and it does get cold at night during the winter months. Nevertheless, getting back to the main subject at hand, some of us Christian folk will go throughout the year praising and worshipping God for all of the things that he has done for us, and then, as soon as these two holidays come rolling around they start to shift that praise to a fat man in a demonic or shall I say a "Magical Flying Sleigh" (which if you ask me are one in the same) and a giant rabbit that gives out eggs! Neither of which have anything to do with Jesus, but we still go along with it because of the Traditions of Men.

In that same sense, let's look at it this way, when Paul said, *"The traditions of men after the basic principles of the world and not according to Christ"*, he was addressing the things that the world does which are the attitudes, the beliefs, and the actions that we as Christians should not practice nor participate in. The reason why we should not practice these things is because they are not rooted and grounded in Jesus Christ. The Tithe, as it is practiced today, is in fact a tradition that does not have its roots in The Law or in Jesus Christ.

How do you think the adversary deceives the Nations when everyone has access to the Word of God? The answer is simple; we do not *"Study to shew thyself approved unto God" (2nd Timothy 2:15)!* We would rather let someone else tell us what the Word of God is instructing us to do instead of ourselves seeking and searching through the Scriptures with the assistance of the one who wrote it, the Holy Spirit. I can remember as a child how we would all get together on Sunday morning and eat breakfast before church. Afterwards, we would all get dressed for church, and before leaving the house we would make sure that we had certain essential items. Chewing gum, check! Money for the offering, check! Handkerchief for sweat and tears, check! But sadly, the Bible was not one of those items. While in church, we would just sit there and listen to the pastor tell stories of being on the mountaintop and seeing the Promised Land, after reading one or two passages of Scripture. After leaving church, most people could not tell you what the message was about to save their life, nor how it would help them in their daily Christian walk. A prime example of this is how many times have we heard that God will,

> *...visit the iniquity of the fathers upon the children to the third and fourth generations.*
> Exodus 20:5/34:7, Numbers 14:18, and Deut 5:9

We have even heard this passage of Scripture used in sermons to justify points of interest that the minister is trying to make concerning sin. Now, to show you how we can so easily be deceived, even using the word of God, let's look at how God changed his mind about these very passages of Scriptures, but you probably have never heard anyone teach it. In Ezekiel 18:19, we see God speaking through Ezekiel the prophet, saying,

> *But if this man begets a son who sees all the sins which his father has done, and fears, and does not do likewise, who does not eat upon the mountains or lift up his eyes to the idols of the house of Israel, does not defile his neighbor's wife, does not wrong any one, exacts no pledge, commits no robbery, but gives his bread to the hungry and covers the naked with a garment, withholds his hand from iniquity, takes no interest or increase, observes my ordinances, and walks in my statutes; he shall not die for his father's iniquity; he shall surely live.*

Continue to read through verse 32 so that your knowledge will override any man's lying spirit. *Let God be true, but every man a liar.* Romans 3:4

"Summation of the Tithe History"

At this point, we are brought to these conclusions:

1) The Tithe was a Tenth of everything that God blessed the Children of Israel with (The Best).

2) It was to be given to the Levites as their inheritance for working as the priests. (Num 18:24)

3) The Levites took out of the Tithe a "Heave Offering," which was a tenth of a tenth, and gave it to Aaron and his sons for their inheritance. (Num 18:25)

4) Aaron would take out of the Heave Offering and pour the blood onto the Altar unto the Lord as a pleasing odor, and eat the flesh. (Num 18:17)

5) Once in the place where God would place his name, the Tithe would be brought to this location or sold for money. There it would be spent on whatever their heart desired. (Deut 12:14-18)

6) The Tithes and offerings were to be brought to Jerusalem or sold, and the money was to be brought there before God to show thanks. (Deut 14:24)

7) The Year of the Tithe was every three years when the Tithe was to be divided among the Levites, strangers, fatherless, and the widows to eat within someone's gates. (Deut 26:12)

8) The storehouse was the place established by God where he placed his name (Jerusalem, in the Temple). (2 Chronicles 6:6)

9) Positions were given out to the people in the city, and the walls were built to keep out those that had no inheritance. (Neh 12:27-13:1)

10) Finally, the commandment to tithe was only for the Children of Israel and the Levites. They were to separate themselves from the ones that had no inheritance from God. (Neh 13:3)

In the next chapter we will be examining what exactly is the LAW, how it affects the followers of Christ, and taking a closer look at the curse from the book of Malachi.

Chapter Two

WHAT IS THE LAW?

The word LAW means an authoritative rule or conduct. In the Bible the word LAW has several different classifications when it is used in the term "The LAW." Some of the classifications are:

    1. The Law of Man—illustrated in Luke 20:22.

    2. The Law written upon the heart—doing things by nature and the conscience also bearing witness, illustrated in Romans 2:15.

    3. The Law—used to express God's will, illustrated in Romans 7:2,9.

    4. The Law—used to represent the entire Old Testament, illustrated in John 10:34.

    5. The Law of Moses—the written Law of Commandments, statutes, and judgments in Deut 6:1.

The LAW of Moses is the primary term that we are concerned with because under it is where the commandment to Tithe was issued (see Hebrews 7:5). Although we know the Practice of the Tithe was started at an earlier date, it is evident that the written commandment was given under the leadership of Moses. To truly understand why there are certain things under The LAW of Moses that we practice today and others that we do not practice, you have to understand the three different parts of The LAW of Moses. These parts are:

1. The Ten Commandments—Deut 5:6.

2. The Statutes—An enactment made by a legislature or LAWS. (There are over 130 of them.)

Pertaining to:

a) Slaves—Numbers 31.

b) Immoral Acts—(Rape, Prostitution, etc.) Deut 22.

c) Marriage for High Priest—(Must marry a virgin that has never been married) Lev 21.

d) Marriage in general—(Not to marry a woman divorced by a man) Deut 24.

e) Inheritance—(How sons inherit their father's estate and not the daughters) Num 27.

f) Sacred Calendar—(Passover, Feast of weeks, and Feast of Tabernacle) Deut 16:9-18.

g) Tithes—Lev 27:30-32/Deut 12:6-17.

3. The Judgments – The act or an instance of imposing Judgment (Blessings/Deut 28:1-14 and Curses/Deut 28:15-68).

"The Law Broken Down"

Consider the purpose of these three distinct sections of The Law of Moses. Paul said in Romans 7:7,

I had not known sin but by the LAW.

The LAW pointed out what sin was because it gave us the basis of what, in God's eyes, was wrong. Not only did it point out what was wrong, but it also pointed out what was right! In order for you to be made righteous under the Law of Moses, you had to do two things: 1) Do not break the Ten Commandments along with all of the other Commandments, 2) Carry out the Statutes or LAWS of the Law of Moses.

I know it sounds like the same thing, but you see, you couldn't just not commit adultery; you also had to Tithe! You couldn't just not steal; you also had to observe the month of A-bib and keep the Passover. You couldn't just not murder; you also had to sanctify the firstling males of your flock. All of these were a combination of parts 1, "The Ten Commandments" and 2, "The Statutes" of the LAW previously listed. If you accomplished all of these things (and I do mean ALL), then part 3, "The Judgments" that would be imposed on you would be what is known as a blessing.   On the other hand, if you were to alleviate something that was written for you to do, then your judgment would be what is known as a curse. In order for one to get a better illustration of how the Law of Moses operated, let's take a look at one of the main parts of the Law, the Blood Sacrifices, Hebrews 9:18,

> *Whereupon not even the First Testament (or Covenant) was dedicated without blood.* Hebrews 9:19, *For when Moses had spoken every precept (or every Commandment) to all the people according to the Law, he took the blood of calves and of goats, with water and*

This was the blood of the first Testament sealing it unto the people, kind of like a final declaration. A Testament is another way of saying covenant or an agreement. This was the First Testament or Agreement between Man and God. God established the seal of any covenant by the shedding of blood. This is evident even within the marriage of a Man and a Woman, for according to the Scriptures when a Man and a Woman are joined physically, they become one flesh. The covenant happens not only at the wedding ceremony but also during intercourse when a woman's hymen rips and blood is shed, therefore consecrating their Covenant with each other. This is the reason why God intended for man to marry before having sex.

So the Priest, every year, would sacrifice animals to use their blood for themselves and the people to remit their sins. Afterwards, the priest was commanded by God to eat the flesh (see Leviticus 6:24). But this way of cleansing was not efficient enough to take the sins away. Notice what Hebrews said in verse 1 of chapter 10.

*For the LAW having a shadow of good things
to come, and not the very image of things, can
never with those sacrifices which they offered
year by year continually make the comers
thereunto perfect.*

You see, according to Hebrews, the LAW was a shadow of things to come. It was all done by the flesh, which is what made it weak. In Romans, chapter 8, verses 3 through 6, Paul best describes why the LAW was fulfilled.

*For what the LAW could not do, in that it was
weak through the flesh, God sending his son*

If you would like to see the list of things that are manifested from walking after the flesh/spirit, see Galatians 5:19. The reason why the righteous requirement can be fulfilled in those that walk after the spirit is because of what Jesus did on Calvary. In Matthew 5:17, Jesus said it best.

*Think not that I am come to destroy the law,
or the prophets: I am not come to destroy, but
to fulfill.*

For us to try and obtain righteousness on our own would be to do as they did under the LAW. But if they could not obtain righteousness by all of their many works of the flesh, what makes us think that we can? I'll go even deeper by saying that if we attempt to be justified by our works or the works of the law then we are telling God that we do not need Jesus and what he did on the cross. No, I'm not talking about putting our Faith to work; what I am talking about is thinking that we can do some kind of work and that work alone will impress God and cause him to bless us, as he did the Children of Israel under the Law.

Some will try and say, "Well, any of the Ten Commandments are still sin if you break them," No kidding! We are not talking about the Ten Commandments; these ten were only a portion of the LAW that the Children of Israel had to practice. What we are addressing here are all of the many different commandments and statutes that were required of them to do, such as Circumcision, or the Law of the Central Sanctuary, or the Law of the firstlings of male flocks. This is why it is stated in Hebrews 7:18 that,

*There is verily a setting aside of the former
Commandments for the weakness and
unprofitablness thereof.*

It would not profit you and me to be under these
Commandments because of two reasons: 1) You and I are
not of Jewish descent, and therefore are not one of the
Children of Israel. God opened redemption up to everyone
on earth. 2) Jesus has done it for us, and all we have to do is
receive his payment by Faith and walk therein. The Tithe is
no different; it was one of the statutes of the LAW and it was
only for the Children of Israel and the Levites. It was not
meant for the Gentiles. Paul said it quite well when he said,

*And by him (Jesus) all that believe are
justified from ALL THINGS from which ye
could not be justified by the Law of Moses.*

You and I fall in this category, because those
commandments of the Law that were just mentioned could
do nothing for you and I in regards to making us righteous in
God's eyes. That was the purpose of the Law. As a matter of
fact, none of the Works of the LAW can, as we see in
Romans 3:20.

*Therefore by the deeds of the LAW there shall
no flesh be justified in his sight: for by the
Law is the knowledge of sin.*

"The Righteous Requirement"

What am I saying? I'm saying this: your
righteousness is made by Jesus and not by the deeds of the
Law. Therefore, by you doing one of the deeds of the Law
and trying to receive something from God because of doing
it, you are spinning your wheels!! Romans 3:28 says,

> *Therefore we conclude that a man is justified
> (or declared righteous) by faith certainly not
> by the deeds of the LAW.*

We can take this even further by saying those that do part of the LAW are bound (or in bondage) to the entire LAW. Galatians 5:3 reads,

> *For I testify again to every man that is
> circumcised, that he is a debtor (or obligated
> to keep) the whole LAW. Christ is become of
> no effect unto you, whosoever of you are
> justified by the law; ye are fallen from grace.*

I am not making this up, Saints of God; this is God's Word that never lies and will never return unto him void! Why do you think Jesus accused the Pharisees and Scribes of being hypocrites for Tithing and not doing the other parts of the Law (Matthew 23:23)? Understand and if not ask God for his wisdom in this matter. After your prayer for his wisdom, read Romans 9:30 all the way to 11:32 so that you can see how God's plan was never meant to just stay the way it was in the Old Testament. *"Christ is the end of the LAW for righteousness to every one that believeth" (10:4).*

You see, Israel was God's chosen people, but God laid a stumbling block for them, which was Christ, and through their unbelief, many will not be saved. Now, if we (Gentiles) were given salvation as a gift from God through Jesus, then how or why would we attempt to gain God's favor by doing the works of the LAW? Now, let's discuss further the righteous requirement of the Law and of Jesus. As Children of God, we have to be righteous before God. In Matthew 25:31-40, we see Jesus speaking to the people of God as he divides the sheep (Christians) from the Goats (Non-Christians). In this passage of Scripture, Jesus refers to the sheep as righteous revealing their high standard as the Body of Christ. Under the Law the righteousness obtained by the Children of Israel was obtained through their works as seen in Deuteronomy 6:25.

*And it shall be our righteousness, if we
observe to do all these commandments before
the Lord our God, as he hath commanded us.*

These things were written under the Law and to the Children of Israel so that they could be made righteous before God. As Christians, our righteousness is measured in Jesus as Paul clearly points out in Philippians 3:8-9.

*That I may win Christ, and be found in him,
not having mine own righteousness, which is
of the Law, but that which is through the
Faith of Christ, the righteousness which is of
God by faith.*

You ask, "what does all of this mean?" It means that we do not obtain righteousness through the Law, but it is obtained in Jesus! It means you and I should not try to be righteous in God's eye by doing the many different commandments, or Works of the Law—like The Law of the Sabbath Year, The Law of the Year of Jubilee, The Law of the Unleavened Bread, The Law of Meats, and the Law of the Tithes as well! As already discussed, the works of the Law were referred to as Fleshly Commandments because they had to be carried out by the flesh (or physically done, i.e., "BRING the Tithe into the Storehouse"). This was the only way to obtain and maintain righteousness in the sight of God. The Levites, which were the chosen priest out of all the tribes of Israel, received their office of priesthood under the LAW. They also have a Commandment of the Law to take the tithes (Hebrews 7:5). Jesus, however, did not receive his office in this manner and therefore is not restricted to the ordinances of the Law, which were all fleshly. According to the author of Hebrews, Jesus, who has come not after the LAW of a Fleshly Commandment, has come after the power of an endless life (Hebrews 7:16). This is why Hebrews states,

*For the priesthood being changed there is
made of necessity a change also of the Law.*

So for those who think that I am trying to change God's word, think again. If you would like to see another key that will open your understanding of what Hebrews is talking about here, just stop right here and take a minute to look at Matthew chapter 5:17. Examine how Jesus took the Law and added to them. Okay, now that you see how Jesus brought the commandments of old into the New Covenant, you should have a clearer understanding of the fulfillment of the Law that you and I have in Jesus. Even if this does not clear things up for you completely, you have to ask yourself, what were the Apostles talking about when they told us to not be under the Law? Were they talking about the Ten Commandments? No, not at all! They still show us what sin is. When Jesus expounded on them, he did it so that our righteousness would exceed that of the Scribes and Pharisees as seen in Matthew 5:19.

So what part of the Law were they talking about? The Apostles were telling us that those more than 130 different works of the Law the Children of Israel were commanded to do for their righteousness are not commandments for followers of Christ. The simple fact is Jesus is our righteousness now and not the works of the Law. Only the Ten Commandments of the Law Jesus took and expounded on are the ones we as Christians (Followers of Christ) should adhere to. We really need to get a grip on this thing. Jesus was the fulfillment of the Law! Since the Law pointed out the Sin, it was still important to Christ's ministry. But he did not just use them; he added to them. These are the things that we as believers should focus on. Now, I am not saying the things in the Old Testament are not worthy of studying, nor am I saying that the things that were spoken by the prophets are not going to come to pass. Jesus himself said, *Not one jot or one title shall pass till all be fulfilled.* But as you can see, he was indeed talking about those prophecies that had not come to pass yet.

"Examples, Not Commandments"

What I am saying is according to Scripture, those things that were written of old are for an example to us as seen in Romans 15:4 and 1st Corinth 10:11. In other words, they are for you and I to study and learn a number of things about the awesome God that we serve and how he interacts with man! Oh sure, if you wanted to follow after some of the Old Commandments that Jesus did not specifically expound on, that's great. To me it would just be a type of dedication that you would do unto the Lord for different reasons. The problem arises when teachers, preachers, Bishops and Apostles of today teach men that these practices are mandatory.

For example, we all know that certain meats were forbidden to eat according to the Law. Now that you and I are under Grace, we are not required to keep this Commandment as illustrated by Jesus in Mark 7:18-19 and seen in 1st Timothy 4:3-5/Romans 14:1-6. But if you wanted to abstain from, let's say, pork, then that would be just fine, as long as you didn't believe and teach men that it has to be so just because it was one of the rules of the Law. This would be your dedication to the Lord, or it could be just for health reasons. Either way, it is not our place to judge our brothers and sisters based on something simple as meat! This is one example of many that are written under the Law and not Commanded of you and me due to the freedom that we have to serve God in Christ Jesus. Paul wrote in Galatians 5:1,

> *Stand fast therefore in the liberty wherewith Christ hath made us free, and be not entangled again with the YOKE OF BONDAGE.*

This is the same area of Scripture mentioned earlier in this chapter. Paul uses the example of Circumcision in an attempt to make everyone understand that believers of Christ are not bound to do these works of the LAW. Circumcision was a very strict and well-practiced part of the LAW that the Children of Israel did to continue in their efforts to remain righteous. We all know and agree that one of the main laws, the Blood Sacrifices, was done away with or fulfilled by Jesus. There were several different types of Sacrifices, but the main one was the Atonement for the Priest, Tabernacle and the People. This Blood Sacrifice was done so that the sins would be covered up and the people would be once again righteous in the sight of God, but it was only a temporary thing. Hebrews 10:1-10 says it best in verse 4.

> *For it is not possible that the blood of bulls and of goats should take away sins. Wherefore when he cometh into the world, he saith, Sacrifice and offering thou wouldest not (or did not desire) but a body hast thou prepared me.*

If you keep on reading this passage of Scripture, you can see it was only a system that was in place until the fullness of time had come that Jesus would be brought on the scene. The Blood of Christ that cleanses the impurities of man totally takes those sins away and not just covers them up. I like the way the author of Hebrews worded it in 9:14.

> *How much more shall the blood of Christ, cleanse your conscience from dead works to serve the living God?*

As you can see, the blood of Christ has done it once and for all making those Laws of Sacrifices none applicable. So you have to ask yourself, if Christ fulfilled the major part of the Law, wouldn't all of the others, in some way, also be fulfilled in him? I think you know as well as I that the answer is crystal clear, Yes! Remember from the chapter "History of the Tithe" how Tithing was directly associated with the sacrifices (Num 18:8-28)? Aaron, and his sons, was the High Priest and received the Heave Offering along with the Firstlings from the Levites. The Levites received this from the Children of Israel (the Tithe) and hence the sacrifices were supplied through this system. So it does not take a rocket scientist to figure out that if the Sacrifices were no longer needed, then the system to supply the sacrifices (the Tithe) are no longer needed as well!

"No Condemnation"

Notice how Paul says, "Cleanse your conscience (or thoughts and convictions) from Dead Works." What do you think he was saying? He is saying that no longer do you nor I have to be condemned because of not doing the works, or as he called them, Dead Works of the Law! Is this not exactly what you feel when someone says to you, "You mean you do not Tithe?" It makes your flesh want to rise up and say, "You mean you do?" Don't let that feeling persuade you into thinking that this is the Holy Spirits conviction because if that were so, it would make what Paul spoke of contradicting. I would even go as far as saying that Paul was telling you and I that we should not even think about doing those Dead Works of the Law, and concentrate on serving the Living God! At this time, I would like to draw your attention to Galatians chapter 3:10 through 25. I will explain what Paul is telling us in a more vivid detail as we go. Verse 10 states,

> *For as many as are of the works of the Law*
> *are under the curse for it is written, CURSED*
> *IS EVERY ONE THAT CONTINUETH NOT*
> *IN ALL THINGS WHICH ARE WRITTEN IN*
> *THE BOOK OF THE LAW TO DO THEM.*

Isn't this exactly what we have been talking about? Throughout the previous chapters, we see that Paul is trying to explain to the Galatians that as followers of Christ we do not have to prove ourselves to God by doing the different works of the Law. As you will notice, Paul uses the circumcision to clearly explain the end of the works of the Law. The reason why he does this is because everyone knows how important the circumcision was. Just as the Tithe, it too was established before, used during and after the Law. But as Paul clearly states throughout the epistles, these commandments of the Law were the very essence of the bondage spoken of by the apostles, as they would try to explain that we are free of these things in Christ. Again, we are not talking about the Ten Commandments; neither are we talking about the things that Jesus taught on that originated in the Law. What we are talking about are all of the many Statutes under the law that were not taught to us by our Lord Jesus. Now, in order for us to distinguish between the two, we simply need to focus on the teachings of Christ because throughout his time on earth, Jesus left nothing up to guess - work.

Getting back to verse 10, Paul is once again trying to show the people that the Law no longer governs them. In fact, Paul was even reminding them of what the Law itself spoke of. That the man who would practice one element of the Law, like Tithing, and not do all of the Law, was indeed cursed. But thanks be to God for verse 13, he said,

> *Christ hath redeemed us from the curse of the Law, being made a curse for us: for it is written, Cursed is every one that hangeth on a tree.* Verse 14, *That the blessing of Abraham might come on the Gentiles (us) through Jesus Christ; that we might receive the promise of the Spirit through faith.*

If you will notice here in verse 14, there are two things that believers of Christ will receive: 1) The Blessing of Abraham, 2) The promise of the Spirit through faith. Not once did Paul mention that the Law or the Tithe under the Law, was the way to receive our blessings, as the Children of Israel received their blessings. There is truly no condemnation in Christ (Romans 8:1)!

"The Law Brought Us to Christ"

Now, a lot of people believe that we are to emulate Abraham in order for us to receive our blessings, but as you can plainly see, the blessing of Abraham, that we as Gentiles were to receive, is in fact received through Jesus Christ. The promise of the spirit is the baptism of the Holy Ghost that Jesus told us would come upon us that BELIEVE IN HIM and give to us power. Let's continue; looking at Galatians 3: 16 through 19, we can really grab a hold of what Paul is saying.

> *Now to Abraham and his SEED (Singular) were the promises made. He saith not, and to SEEDS (Plural) as of many; but as of one, and to thy seed, which is Christ. And this I say, that the covenant, that was confirmed before of God in Christ (Grace) the Law, which was four hundred and thirty years after, cannot disannul, that it (The Law) should make the promise (Grace) of none effect. For if the inheritance be of the Law, it is no more of promise: but God gave it to Abraham by promise. Wherefore then serveth the Law? It was ADDED because of transgressions, TILL THE SEED SHOULD COME to whom the promise was made.*

Paul is saying that the promise made to Abraham would actually come into existence through his seed, which was Jesus Christ. The Law was merely added because of sin so that there would be a tutor or watchman that would keep the people until the promise would come. You see, we have had this mentality that the Law was first and foremost and that Jesus was God's backup plan, but that is all wrong. God's plan for us was redemption through his Son, Jesus, and the Law was God's way of showing man how redemption would come. In verses 23 through 25, Paul confirms this by explaining,

> *But before faith came, we were kept under the Law, shut up unto the faith which should afterwards be revealed. Wherefore the Law was our schoolmaster to bring us unto Christ, that we might be justified by faith. BUT AFTER THAT FAITH IS COME, WE ARE NO LONGER UNDER A SCHOOLMASTER.*

I think Paul summed all of this up in verses 28 and 29 when he said,

> *For ye are all one in Christ Jesus. And if ye be Christ's, then are ye Abraham's seed, and heirs according to the promise.*

This is an interesting phrase that Paul used, *heirs according to the promise.* Not according to the Works of the Law but according to the promise, which is the spirit of God through Jesus Christ. This is why, once you accept what Jesus has done on the cross, the Law with its condemnation does not condemn you anymore. This is why if you ask someone, "Will I be in sin because I do not Tithe?" He or she cannot say, "Yes, you are in sin!" If they do, tell them to read the above scriptures because Tithing is of the Law!

"The Judgments of the Law"

The last part of the Law that we are going to examine in our quest to reveal exactly what the Law was is the <u>Judgments of the Law</u>. In Deuteronomy, chapter 27:9-10, we see this picture of Moses standing before the Children of Israel issuing out God's Commandments. When Moses had finished giving out all of the Commandments of the LAW that God had given him, he and the priest (The Levites) spoke to all of Israel, saying,

*Thou shalt therefore obey the voice of the
Lord thy God, and do his Commandments and
his statutes which I command thee this day.*

Notice how the Tithe was just mentioned over in verse 12 of chapter 26. In verse 11 of chapter 27, we see Moses placing six of the sons of Israel (Jacob) on the Mount of Ger-i-zim to bless the people as they walk by, and on the other side, on Mount E'-bal, Moses placed the other six sons of Israel (Jacob) to proclaim the curses as the people would walk by. These blessings and curses had to be spoken over the people so that in the event of obedience or disobedience, the proper judgment would be initiated. This also was a way of proclaiming the judgments of God to the people. There were almost three times as many curses than there were blessings, which show us how serious God was about his people maintaining a righteous state. The only way to do this under the Law was to keep all of the Commandments as seen in chapter 6:25. The one curse in particular that we are concerned with is the 12th curse that reads,

*Cursed be he that confirmeth not all the
words of this Law to do them. And all the
people shall say, Amen.*

You see it is this curse that condemned the Children of Israel. It was this curse that set the standard by stating that if a person did not do all that was written in the Law, they were cursed. When you look at Malachi 3:6-12, you see God telling them that they were cursed with a curse because the people had gone away from God's Commandments. This means that they were not doing ALL of what God had written and commanded them to do in the Law—The Law of Moses that stated a person had to obey all of the Commandments and Statutes so that they would remain in good standing with the Almighty. If the people were obedient, then their Judgment would be the Blessings of God, if they were disobedient, then their Judgment would be the Cursings. But God said that these people, in the book of

Malachi, had gone away from his Commandments, *Even from the days of your Fathers,* which meant that going all the way back to when Moses had given out the Commandments of God, there were those that did not keep them. So therefore, this curse that is mentioned in Malachi verse 9, *"Cursed with a Curse",* is the exact, same curse that was issued and spoken over the Children of Israel in Deuteronomy chapter 27:26. We can see, by looking at chapter 28:18, That the curse in the book of Malachi is directly linked to the curse from the Law by comparing the actions of the curse. Let us compare these two Scriptures. In the book of Malachi, God told the people that if they would return unto him by returning unto his Law, then he would rebuke the devourer from destroying the fruits of the people's land. Also he said that neither shall your vine fail to bear fruit for you in the field. Now, let's look back at the stipulations of the curse in the Law. Deuteronomy chapter 28:16/18 reads,

> *Cursed shalt thou be in the city, and cursed shalt thou be IN THE FIELD. Verse 18, Cursed shall be the fruit of thy body, and the FRUIT OF THY LAND.*

As you can plainly see, the curse that is mentioned in Malachi is in fact the same curse that Moses instructed the sons of Jacob to proclaim over the people for not obeying all of the commandments of the Law. Let's conduct another comparison. In Malachi 3:10, God told the people,

> *Prove me now herewith, saith the Lord of hosts, if I WILL NOT OPEN YOU THE WINDOWS OF HEAVEN.*

Now, in keeping with this promise, let's look back at another stipulation in the curse of the LAW. In Deut 28:23, God said,

> *AND THY HEAVEN THAT IS OVER THY HEAD SHALL BE BRASS.*

This clearly illustrates how the promises in Malachi for obedience are directly related to the Curses spoken over the Children of Israel for their disobedience. The curse in Malachi is simply a quote from the curse of the Law!

The Tithe, in the book of Malachi, is not the only Commandment of the Law that the people had gone away from, but it is the only one that is quoted today. The priests despised the name of the Lord, the people committed idolatry and they divorced for any reason. So it is evident that because of their disobedience to God's word in all of these areas, their Judgment, according to the proclaimed curses of the Law, would come upon them if they did not return unto God. By reading the book of Malachi, we see that God was trying to bring the people back unto him; back to practicing all of the Law and not just certain things. But thanks be to God for his ultimate plan for our salvation. A plan that not only delivers us from what Paul described as *"Dead Works"*, but it also redeemed you and I from the Curse of the Law. I don't know about you, but I thank God for Jesus!

Chapter Three

THE LAW AND GRACE CANNOT COEXIST

Understanding that the Law of Moses' purpose was to identify sin and to give mankind a standard to live by is only the beginning. From the time Adam sinned until God gave Moses his commandments, the world did not have any guidance, and mankind did whatever felt right. God chose Israel to be his people because of the faith displayed in Abraham. The promise to Abraham made by God is, and always was, through the Grace given in our Lord Jesus Christ. The Law of Moses was only an institution of laws given to the Children of Israel to make them a Holy People unto God until the coming of Christ; therefore, once Christ had come, there was no longer a need to follow those statutes and laws for the purpose of righteousness. Considering the flow of these events that led the world to Christ, it is evident that the Law and Grace cannot exist at the same time!

What this means is that you can either place yourself totally under the Law, or totally under the Grace of God given in our Lord and Savior Jesus Christ. The Tithe thus far has been clearly pointed out in the previous chapters as being one of the commandments of the LAW. Everyone that has a general understanding of the LAW can recite to you some, if not all, of the Ten Commandments, but what about the other commandments like the Tithe? When you really look at it, in comparison with let's say Stoning, Tithing is just as much a part of the LAW as anything else. How many church services have you been in lately where they sacrificed a sheep for a heave offering, and the preacher, who better be a Levite, poured out the blood on the altar and ate the meat there in the presence of the Lord? You haven't; I hope! Therefore, why are we still trying to justify ourselves through the works of the LAW when we as born-again Christians are saved by grace in which is the only way to receive blessings from God the Father.

According to Scripture, the Law had become a form of bondage that the apostles spoke of on several different occasions. The Jews that lived during the time of Jesus and the Disciples/Apostles were still living according to the Law of Moses. It was a constant battle for the Disciples to not only teach people about Christ, but to break them away from the practices involved in the Law. Let's take a look at what Paul said to the Romans in chapter 10 about Israel.

> *Brethren, my hearts desire and prayer to God for Israel is, that they might be saved. For I being their witness that they have a zeal for God, but not according to knowledge for they being ignorant of God's righteousness, and going about to establish their own righteousness, have not submitted themselves unto the righteousness of God. For Christ is the end of the LAW for righteousness to everyone that believeth. For Moses describeth the righteousness which is of the LAW, that the man which doeth those things shall live by them.*

Paul said, *For they being ignorant of God's righteousness*. This is Israel we are talking about; they are ignorant of God's righteousness, which we know is Jesus Christ. They were doing their own thing to establish righteousness and would not submit themselves unto what God had established for them. In the 4th and 5th verses, you see Paul comparing the righteousness, which is of the LAW, to that which is in Christ Jesus, and as Paul was pointing out here I agree; there is no comparison! In the next couple of Scriptures, Paul quoted Moses when he said that the man which doeth those THINGS (of the LAW) shall live by them. He did not say that you could pick and choose which one of the things of the LAW that you can do and live by; he was talking about the whole thing. Remember, the righteousness of the LAW came from doing all of it not just one part. That would be like saying that you only want part of the righteousness given in Christ! In other words, you either practice all of the LAW and live by it, or you practice none of it at all. Many of us in the Body of Christ are in the same situation as Israel was, in that we are still trying to follow after our own beliefs. We try to follow after what we think that we must do out of God's word and not after what our Lord and Savior Jesus Christ commanded us to do. In Romans chapter 7:5-6, Paul said,

> *For when we were in the flesh, the passions of sins, which were by the LAW, did work in our members to bring forth fruit unto death, but now we are delivered from the LAW, that we being dead wherein we were held; that we should serve in newness of spirit, and not in the oldness of the Letter.*

This passage of Scripture is like a sunbeam breaking through a thick dark group of clouds that hover over our Christian walk. Paul said for us to *"Serve in newness of spirit, and not in the oldness of the Letter,"* speaking of the Letter of the LAW. If you were in the state penitentiary for a crime, every day you would have certain chores to do. You would accomplish these chores so that your sentence would be easier, as opposed to making your sentence harder by not doing the things that you were told to do. But when your time served was complete and you were released from jail, you would no longer be held responsible for the chores you did while inside. You wouldn't get up every day and go back to the jail so that you could do those chores that you did while you were there, would you? Of course not, now that you are outside or no longer under the Laws governing the penitentiary, you would be expected to follow the Laws established by the local city and state that you would reside in. This is what Paul is telling us; we should no longer serve God under the old LAW, but that we should serve God in newness of spirit in Christ Jesus! The problem with the Body of Christ is the same as that of the Children of Israel; we are afraid of the change that is associated with breaking away from the law and entering the freedom in Christ Jesus! That is why Paul wrote in 2nd Corinth 3:13-16,

> *Seeing then that we have such hope, we use great boldness of speech: And not as Moses, which put a vail over his face, that the children of Israel could not steadfastly look to the end of that which is abolished:* **But their minds were blinded: for until this day remaineth the same vail untaken away in the reading of the old testament; which vail is done away in Christ. But even unto this day, when Moses is read, the vail is upon their heart.** *Nevertheless when one shall turn to the Lord, the vail shall be taken away.*

To truly understand that the Disciples as well as the Apostle Paul knew there was a distinction to be made between being under the Law and being under Grace, let's look at the author of our faith—Jesus! Jesus himself had the same problem with the Jewish people that followed the law. They did not receive him as the Son of God because he did not follow their image of how the Messiah should be. They expected the Messiah that was to come to be one that followed the law and teachings of Moses and Abraham, even though they themselves did not. But Jesus was not a follower of man! Jesus is not only the Son of God in the flesh, but also God's very word in the flesh, which means Jesus has always been in existence. In the book of John 8, we see Jesus having a debate with the Pharisees over who Jesus is. The Pharisees did not believe in Jesus and sought to trap him in his actions and words concerning who Jesus said that he was. Jesus spoke boldly to the Pharisees about himself, explaining to them that he is the light of the world, but most would not receive him. They tried everything from accusing him of bearing false witness to being filled with a demon. But notice what Jesus said to them about being free.

> *We be Abraham's seed, and were never in bondage to any man: how sayest thou, Ye shall be made free?* John 8:33

They did not understand what Jesus was saying, which was nothing new because rarely did they understand our Lord. Remember the veil that was mentioned? Well, that veil was symbolic of a blockage that stopped the Jewish people from understanding the things of God because of their own actions (read Romans 1:21-32/2). God even said that he laid a stumbling block for them, which was Jesus himself (read Isaiah 8:1-14)! So the people did not understand that this freedom Jesus spoke of was himself. We are not ruled by the law or of sin. It is in Jesus that we receive the spirit of God. The spirit of God keeps us and delivers us from the sin that is identified in the law (Romans 6:1-14). Jesus is the yoke that breaks all bondage including that of the law.

The Disciples tried to explain that the freedom we have in Jesus sets us free from the law. Once in the book of the Acts of the Apostles, Peter spoke out against the people wanting them to return to the works of the Law in the area of circumcision (Acts 15:6-11). Again, we see this in the epistle to the Galatians when Paul points out that the entire Law was indeed a form of bondage by using the example of circumcision. He wrote in chapter 4:21-31 and chapter 5:1-4,

> *Tell me, ye that desire to be under the Law, DO YE NOT HEAR THE LAW? For it is written, that Abraham had two sons, the one by a bondmaid (Ishmael) the other by a freewoman (Isaac). But he who was of the bondwoman (Ishmael) was born after (or according to) the flesh; but he of the*

freewoman was by promise. Which things are an allegory (or symbolic) for these are the two covenants (the Law-A'-gar, Grace-Sarah); the one from the mount Si'-nai (The Law of Moses) which gendereth (or gives birth to) BONDAGE, which is A'-gar. For this A'-gar is mount Si'-nai in Arabia, and corresponds to Jerusalem which now is, and is in bondage with her children. Verse 28, Now we, brethren, as Isaac was, are the children of promise. But as then he that was born after the flesh persecuted him that was born after the Spirit, even so it is now. Nevertheless what saith the scripture? CAST OUT THE BONDWOMAN AND HER SON (or the Law and her bondage) FOR THE SON OF THE BONDWOMAN SHALL NOT BE HEIRWITH THE SON OF THE FREEWOMAN (or the Promise of the spirit). So then, brethren we are not children of the bondwoman (or children of the Law) but of the free (children of the spirit). Stand fast therefore in the LIBERTY wherewith Christ hath made us free, and BE NOT ENTAGLED AGAIN WITH THE "YOKE OF BONDAGE." Behold, I Paul say unto you, that if ye be circumcised, Christ shall profit you nothing. For I TESTIFY AGAIN to every man that is CIRCUMCISED, that HE is a debtor to do the whole LAW. Christ is become of no effect unto you, whosoever of you are justified by the Law; YE ARE FALLEN FROM GRACE.

Now, I know this is a lot of ground to cover, but I feel that this is very important for you to understand. Paul is telling us that A'-gar and Mount Si'-nai both gave birth to bondage, which were Ishmael and the Law. Jerusalem is in bondage with her children because they are living according to the Law, but she herself is free. However, we that are born of the Spirit, which is symbolized here by Isaac who was born of a freewoman (Sarah), are free. Free, meaning that we are not under the bondage of the Law, as they were, with its fleshly commandments (or things that had to be done by the flesh in order to be justified in the eyes of God). We are children of the Spirit, made to be justified in the eyes of God by what his Son did on the cross, not by what we can do in the flesh, such as being circumcised.

So if circumcision was indeed a yoke of bondage from before, during and after the Law, then the Tithe is no different. What I am trying to show you is that both of these commandments were established before the Law as well as being practiced during the Law and afterwards. Remember how Abraham paid Tithes to Melchizedek and later he circumcised himself and his entire house? Well, these two practices started with Abraham and were later given to the Children of Israel by Moses. Now, the very act of being circumcised is not going to cause you to fall from grace. If that were the case, then a lot of men, including myself, would be in trouble! But if someone were to read this commandment and have it done so that they would be justified in God's eyes, then they would fall in this category of being fallen from grace. Why? Because by doing this that person is going back to the provisions of the Law in order to be justified in the sight of God. No longer do they believe God's word that it is by Grace that we are saved; they are now trying to earn or to keep their righteousness by the deeds of the Law. So if this is true for circumcision, then what makes the Tithe any different? How can we "cookie cut" the Scriptures by practicing one and not the other? If you wanted to give ten percent to your local church, then there is nothing wrong with that (again, it would be kind of a personal standard or even a dedication). But, on the other hand, if you were doing it because of the same reason in the example above, then now you are trying to be justified by this work of the Law. You are saying to God, "I do not need to have faith in Jesus for my increase. I can receive from God directly by my work of the Law in the Tithe."

"Satan's Plan"

Paul warned us in Colossians 2:8-9,

> *Beware lest any MAN take you captive through philosophy and empty deceit, according to the tradition of men, after the basic principles of the world, and not according to Christ.*

Not every man that stands in a sanctuary, that broadcasts on a radio, or even that writes a book, is sent by God. When Paul mentioned philosophy and empty deceit, according to the traditions of men, don't let it fool you into believing that someone cannot take God's word and twist it to deceive you; in fact, this is Satan's plan so that just as Jesus said, *"THERE ARE TARES GROWING UP WITH THE WHEAT"*. The deception that is mentioned throughout the Bible is not just confounded to the world, but in essence it is mostly found in the church! I'm not condemning anyone that is preaching the Tithe, especially the members of the Five Fold Ministry. There are a lot of greatly anointed men and women of God out there, but there are also those that have allowed Satan to deceive them. We all know that there are things within the word of God that have not even been revealed to man yet because God's word is a living word. That is why Paul wrote in Ephesians 3:2-4,

> *If ye have heard of the stewardship of the grace of God which is given me to you-ward: How that by revelation he made known unto me the mystery (or hidden truth); (as I wrote before in few words, Whereby, when ye read, ye may understand my knowledge in the mystery of Christ).*

On the other hand, we must not forget that just because we are saved and filled with the Holy Spirit, or that because we prophesy and move in the different gifts, that we cannot be deceived and lead others astray. The word specifically tells us that the Gifts and Callings of God are without repentance. That means once you got it, you got it! There are people in the church that have been there for years and move freely in the gifts, but have sin in their life and are fully aware of it! A drunken bum on the street can speak a word of knowledge! But deception is one of Satan's greatest tools. He uses it to get people sidetracked so that we think everything is fine and then he comes along and wipes us out.

Remember what Jesus said in Matthew 24:24.

> *For there shall arise false Christs, and false prophets, and shall shew great signs and wonders; insomuch that, if it were possible, they shall deceive the very elect.*

Now, I know that some of this Scripture references the spirit of the Anti-Christ, but there is also Scripture that points to the very saints of God! They thought they were in good standing with Jesus, but they were sadly mistaken!

> *Many will say to me in that day, Lord, Lord, have we not prophesied in thy name? And in thy name have cast out devils? And in thy name done many wonderful works? And then will I profess unto them, I never knew you: depart from me, ye that work iniquity.*
> Matthew 7:22

In 1st Peter, chapter 5, verse 8, Paul warns us again by saying,

> *Be sober, be vigilant (OR ON THE LOOK OUT); because your adversary the devil, as a roaring lion, walketh about, seeking whom he MAY devour.*

This is not to say that we should be afraid because God has not given us a spirit of fear, but we need to be aware of the tricks of the enemy as well as the fruit of the flesh. Even though the Tithe is not practiced as it was in the Law, the complete principle behind the Tithe is preached. The motivation behind the Tithe today is that of a monetary value. This includes both using the blessings and cursings to instill a false sense of security and fear.

"Saved by Grace"

Considering that we are saved by GRACE we are delivered from the law having died with Christ, to that which we were held by, we should serve God in newness of spirit and not in the oldness of the letter (Romans 7:6). The Law can only point out what in God's eyes is considered sin (The Ten Commandments), but it cannot save; therefore, it cannot destroy (Speaking of the other Statues of the Law). That means that the Law in itself does not have the ability to save nor destroy us. This is why, through Jesus Christ, the Grace of God saves us, and by not following him and receiving him we are destroyed! Have you ever wondered what exactly the Grace of God is? Grace is the undeserving love of God in which not only did he give us his Son so that we might be saved, but he is also giving everyone that has not excepted Jesus time to do so. As we all know, Jesus is the only way that you and I can become righteous in God's sight. We cannot achieve this by doing the different works of the LAW. In John 3:16-17, a widely quoted passage of Scripture, we have a clear picture of how much God loves us. It also illustrates how Jesus is the only way we can be saved.

For God so loved the world that he gave his only begotten son that whosoever believeth in him should not perish, but have everlasting life. For God sent not his son into the world to condemn the world; but that the world through HIM might be saved.

Notice how the works of the LAW are not even mentioned here as any part of the plan for salvation. Therefore, I have no other choice than to state for the record, if the LAW cannot save, how can by doing the Works of the LAW bless us? IT CANNOT! We must keep in mind that our relationship with God the Father is by Faith and through the Grace given in our Lord Jesus Christ. There is nothing that the LAW can do for us except show us what sin is, reveal to us the prophecies that have not come to pass yet, and to be an example of God's mighty works. Our works should line up with the teachings of Christ and not those of the law! Until we understand this, we will not be able to properly receive from God.

Paul spoke of the promise made to Abraham in the 4th chapter of Romans, verse 13; he said,

> *For the promise that he should be the heir of the world, was not to Abraham or to his seed through the LAW, but through the righteousness of Faith.*

We know that the righteousness of Faith is Jesus Christ, which is the only way to receive the promise of everlasting life. You have to sincerely ask yourself, would God establish a New Covenant with us and retain statutes from the Old Covenant? Well, the answer is NO! Hebrews 8:7 reads,

> *For if the first covenant had been faultless, then should no place have been sought for the second. For finding fault with them, he (God) saith behold, the days come saith the lord, when I will make a New Covenant with the house of Israel and with the house of Judah (The tribe that Jesus came from): NOT ACCORDING TO THE COVENANT THAT I*

The New Covenant mentioned in this Scripture was part of a direct quote from the Old Testament concerning Jesus Christ. This New Covenant would take the place of the old one and God even said that the new one would not be according to the old one! You can find the majority of this prophecy's fulfillment in Matthew chapter 5, which makes this crystal clear; the New Covenant will have nothing to do with the Old one, that everything in the new one is exactly what it says, a New Covenant! Now, we know that Jesus said in Matthew, chapter 5, verse 17,

*Think not that I'm come to destroy the LAW,
or the prophets: I'm come not to destroy but
to fulfill.*

I know that this Scripture has been repeated several times within the pages of this book, but it is so imperative that it sinks into your good ground. Jesus was simply saying here that both the LAW and the prophets were directing us to the coming of Jesus Christ. This is why he said, *I'm come not to destroy but to FULFILL!* I believe that this is another passage of Scripture that is either misunderstood to mean we are still to obey the different parts of the LAW, or it is being misused to justify the commandment of Tithing from the LAW. Nevertheless, by understanding now what Jesus is saying here, we can plainly see that Jesus was the manifestation of some prophecies of old and the fulfillment of the LAW. Let's look at the next verse, 18.

*For verily I say unto you, till heaven and
earth pass, one jot or one title shall in no wise
pass from the LAW, TILL ALL BE
FULFILLED.*

Need I say more? It is so clear what Jesus is saying here; there are two parts of the LAW that Jesus was addressing: (1) The prophets which lived during and under the LAW in which the prophecies came forth from God. (2) The written LAW, which was all of the commandments and statues. Concerning the prophets, Jesus said that he did not come to destroy them but to fulfill them, meaning that all of the prophecies that spoke of a messiah pointed to the time of Christ. Therefore, he being the Christ had fulfilled these prophecies. The written LAW, or Commandments, statutes, and judgments are in the same fulfillment as the prophets in that by the coming of Jesus no one is any longer held accountable for practicing and completing all of the many parts of the LAW. That through Jesus this requirement is fulfilled. In verse 18, Jesus points out that nothing from the LAW shall pass until all is fulfilled, which again he is addressing those things that have been spoken of but have not come to pass yet. But take a look again at verse 17, Jesus said that he has come to fulfill it; do you see that revelation? He is talking about such things like the Abomination of Desolation from the book of Daniel 9:27, or the taking away (Rapture) of the church in Matthew 24:40 and 1st Corinth 15:51-52. These things had not happened as of the time that Jesus was here on Earth; therefore, they were prophecy that would indeed come to pass one day.

In Matthew 5:19, immediately after the revelation of the law being fulfilled, we see Jesus establishing the LAWS of the New Covenant. If you ask me, it seems only fair that Jesus was given the authority to add to the Ten Commandments; after all, he is the Son and Word of God! If you were selected by Congress to pay a fine in order for everyone in the United States to be set free from the LAW that was currently in effect, wouldn't it be only fair that you and you alone were allowed to rewrite the LAWS? This is exactly what God has allowed Jesus to do; he came to earth to give his blood, body and life as full payment for the sins of the world that broke God's LAW. But now we have an even better covenant through grace. Remember what Paul said in Romans chapter 5, verse 14,

*For if they which are of the LAW be heirs,
Faith is made void, and the promise made of
none effect.*

Paul is telling us here that there is only one way to receive the promise of God! So you can go out and attempt to obtain your own righteousness under the LAW or accept the righteousness of God, which is the grace given in Jesus. Choose you this day!

If I'm not mistaken, Jesus himself answered this question in John 14:6.

*I'm the way, the truth, and the life: no man
cometh unto the Father, but by me.*

Wouldn't this also mean that trying to come unto the Father to receive by way of something outside of Jesus and his teachings, be an alternate route to God? Jesus did not tell us to Tithe so that we may receive; Jesus told us to give and then we would receive. So why don't we all stop trying to justify the Tithe, which was according to the LAW! We need to accept the fullness of the blessings of God, which we can only receive by our Faith in his word and the teachings of his only begotten Son, Jesus Christ, which is one in the same!

Have you noticed how people who proclaim the Tithe is for today will use the prominence of Abraham, Moses, and Melchizedek to justify their beliefs? In this next section we will be looking at these three individuals that the author of Hebrews clearly describe as not being superior to Christ. But I still find myself wondering, how can anyone who claim salvation even consider this to be so?

"Is Abraham Superior to Christ?"

Some have said that Abraham established the Tithe, and since he was alive before the LAW the Tithe should be still in effect. Well, it is true that he was alive and that he did Tithe before the Law was written, as we have already discussed in the earlier parts of this book. However, to say that Abraham established the Tithe would mean that Abraham was the creator of the Tithe. That it was all his idea and he should even receive the glory. We know that the word of God tells us every good and perfect gift is from above and in order for the LAW to be written down as a consolidated set of instructions, man received them individually in different ways. Some, as in the case of Abraham, received them in their minds and hearts from God, and then they were eventually written down after years of being practiced.

It is explained to us in vivid detail how this could have happened. Hebrews chapter 1, verse 1, reads,

> *God who in many portions and in many ways*
> *spake in time past unto the fathers by the*
> *prophets.*

This is a clear explanation of how and why Abraham started Tithing before the Law, and later on it was placed in the LAW. Hebrews states, *"God who in many portions and in many ways"*. The word portions here means bits and pieces of information. The term *"MANY WAYS"* tell us that God used a variety of things to speak unto the Fathers of old by way of the prophets. No one knows exactly when and by whom did Abraham receive the idea of the Tithe, but as this Scripture reads, Father Abraham had to have received it from one of God's MANY WAYS! In verse 2,

> *Hath in these last days spoken to us by his*
> *son.*

You see, God now speaks to us by his Son in whom we should obey what he taught us and not mimic the actions of Father Abraham. We can learn a lot about having faith in God by observing Father Abraham's works, but that is not to say that we should follow him because we could also learn the same thing from studying the lifestyle of Job! If there is any person, we are to follow and live according to the way they lived, then that person is none other than Jesus Christ! In verse 1 of the second chapter, it is reiterated that,

> *Therefore we ought to give the more earnest heed to the things which we have heard, lest at anytime we should drift away.*

The things that we have heard are the things that Jesus taught on throughout his ministry here on earth. By sticking to those things that Jesus taught to us, Hebrews is saying that we should not drift away from the truth if we do not allow ourselves to stray. Continuing on, we see how it was really stressed to the people that Jesus is in all manners higher than anyone that they recognized as having power and authority. In verses 4 through 6,

> *Being made so much better than the Angels, as he hath by inheritance obtained a more excellent NAME THAN THEY.* Verse 5, *For unto which of the Angels said he (God) at any time, thou art my son, this day have I begotten thee?* Verse 6, *And again when he bringeth in the first begotten into the world, he saith, and let all the ANGELS of God worship him (Jesus).*

God said that even the Angels shall worship Jesus, along with all of the prophets who are also in subjection to him. The Tithe was given to the Children of Israel as a commandment years after it started with Abraham, but it was still a part of the LAW and created by God. Besides, if there were things that Abraham started, they were all added to the written LAW such as the burnt offerings, sacrifices and the circumcision. Then in turn, the coming of Christ and his New Commandments fulfilled the LAW. Some of the Law was fulfilled and done away with while Jesus expounded on other parts such as the ones talked about in Matthew 5. By saying the commandment to Tithe is justified because it was started by Abraham would be the same as saying that

Abraham is superior to Christ. Why else would someone say that we should Tithe because of Abraham, if they were not telling you and I that Abraham is indeed superior to Christ? Therefore, we should not be living according to what Abraham might have started, but we should be concentrating on the commandments given to us by our Lord and Savior, Jesus Christ!!!

"Is Moses Superior to Christ?"

In chapter 3:1 through 6, it compares Moses with Jesus,

> *Wherefore, holy brethren, partakers of the heavenly calling, consider the Apostle and High Priest of our confession, Christ Jesus; who was faithful to him that appointed him, as also Moses was faithful in all his house. For this man (Christ) was counted worthy of more glory than Moses, inasmuch as he who hath builded the house hath more honor than the house. For every house is builded by some man; but he that built all things is God.*

You see, Jesus Christ, according to the book of John, was the word of God, which is one of the three manifestations of God (God the Father, Son/Word, Holy Spirit). The Word was in the beginning with God as well as actually being God, so therefore Jesus Christ in the Spirit was God and built all things.

In verses 5 and 6 it reads,

> *And Moses verily was faithful in all his house, as a servant, for a testimony of those things which were to be spoken afterward; But Christ as a son over his own house; whose house are we if we hold fast the confidence*

and the rejoicing of the hope firm unto the
end.

You see, Hebrews is saying that Moses and everyone in his house were faithful to God, and we as the Body of Christ represents Christ's house whom by also being faithful unto the end will receive our reward. The understanding here is that Jesus is superior to Moses as well as Abraham, but you don't see Christians (followers of Christ) sentencing a man to death because he raped someone (even though our flesh would probably agree to doing this). But this was the procedure written under the LAW of Moses (Deuteronomy 22:25). So why are some justifying the practice of Tithing after The Law of Moses? It is because of the superiority of Jesus over the commandments of the Law that we do not condemn anyone for their sins as compared to the condemnation of the Law (Luke 9:56 is an example of this).

"Is Melchizedek Superior to Christ?"

Now, let's take a look at a man in the Bible, that had a Priesthood and nature of which is a "Christ-Like" figure, named Melchizedek. Melchizedek was the High Priest to whom the Patriarch Abraham paid a tenth of his spoils. In the seventh chapter of Hebrews, it gives us a description of this Melchizedek; he was a High Priest of God that lived in the days of Abraham. This Melchizedek was, *Without mother, without father, without descent, having neither beginning of days, nor end of life; but made like unto the Son of God.* Now, this is not to say that Melchizedek was immortal, no not at all; it just means that there is no record of this man's parents, birth or of his death. What the author of Hebrews is doing here is trying to establish the relationship of Melchizedek to Jesus' priesthood. I guess you are wondering, what does all of this have to do with tithing? Well, if we look in the next two verses, you will see. Verses 4 and 5 say,

Now that may sound like a bunch of gibberish to you, but actually it is setting us up for what we are really looking for. You see, the commandment to Tithe was given under the Law, which at the time of Abraham and Melchizedek's day, it had not been written. Nevertheless, Abraham paid Tithes to Melchizedek who was not a High Priest under the Law neither was he a descendent of the Tribe of Levi, considering Levi was still in the loins of Abraham. The author of Hebrews had to establish these facts in order for the Hebrews to understand what he was trying to point out to them.

Melchizedek was said by the Bible to be *Christ Like,* but the Word of God does not say that he was Christ, so let's get that straight right now! The word also said that this Melchizedek is "A Priest Continually." Jesus himself was quoted as being *A Priest forever according to the order of Melchizedek.* So what was *The Order of Melchizedek* that Jesus was made a Priest after? Well, let's look at it and see. In Hebrews 7:2-3, we see that Melchizedek,

nor end of life but resembling the Son of God
he continues a priest forever.

As you can see, the order that Jesus was to be a Priest afterwards was that like Melchizedek, Jesus is also translated as being the King of Righteousness, Peace, and he is without Genealogy. The reason Jesus' Genealogy cannot be truly traced is because he did not come from the seed of man but from God's seed. It was the Holy Spirit that overshadowed Mary, and she conceived (Luke 1:30-35), so how can you trace God's genealogy? You can't! The genealogy for Jesus that is mentioned in the Bible is that of Mary's husband Joseph (Matthew 1:1-16). Joseph's genealogy goes back to the Tribe of Judah which came from Jacob who was renamed "Israel." Now, the Scripture says that Melchizedek was made like the Son of God. Why? Well, mostly due to the above translations, but it is also because there is not a record of Melchizedek's birth or of his death. We know that Jesus was born in the flesh and died on Calvary, but we also know that Jesus is the very word of God that was made into flesh to dwell with us (John 1:14). He was the ultimate living sacrifice for our sins! Remember John said in Revelation 5:6, *I saw a Lamb standing, as though it had been slain.* The Word of God was in the beginning with God; therefore, Jesus was there as well. I mean whom do you think God was talking to in Genesis when he said, *Let US make Man in OUR image* and again at the Tower of Babel when God said, *Let us go down, and there confound their language*?

Now, Jesus' death was also noted as being a temporary thing because now he sits at the right hand of the Father forever. Melchizedek has no record of his death, and the Bible says therefore that he is a priest forever since no one knows when nor if he died; thus is the order of Melchizedek! The author was not telling the Hebrews that Jesus should receive Tithes from us, as Melchizedek did from Abraham, and anyone who is using this to justify Tithing is absolutely wrong (Hebrews 9:25-28)! The author of Hebrews was simply using the stature of this man,

Melchizedek, to show the Hebrews that Jesus was much more of a High Priest than he. Melchizedek was well known to the people because they had studied him from generation to generation. The author of Hebrews knew this and was using the story of Melchizedek to show them how a High Priest back then, who was not of the Levitical Priesthood, was so highly esteemed that Abraham paid Tithes to him. He further illustrates this by saying that even the entire Priesthood of the Levites paid Tithes to him seeing that they were from the seed of Abraham and was in his loins at the time Abraham paid Tithes to Melchizedek.

The point that he was making is evident in Hebrews 7:14 when he said,

> *For it is evident that our Lord was descended from Judah, and in connection with that tribe Moses said nothing about priests. This becomes even more evident when another priest arises in the likeness of Melchizedek who has become a priest, not according to a legal requirement concerning bodily descent but by the power of an indestructible life. For it is witnessed of him Thou art a priest for ever, after the order of Melchizedek.*

A priest forever according to the order of Melchizedek because again Jesus did not come from the Tribe of Levi, which is where the Priesthood derived from, and neither did Melchizedek! There is not any record of Melchizedek's death, which means he is a priest continually. Jesus sits at the right hand of God and is a High Priest forever. Now, some will still use this Scripture to justify Tithing, but now that your knowledge has increased, you have enough ammo from the Word of God to spark your curiosity and to test every spirit (1 John 4:1).

You now know the history of the Tithe; you know that its purpose was for an inheritance of the High Priest Aaron and the Levites; you also know that it was the supply for the blood sacrifice, and you know that Jesus is our High Priest forever after the order of Melchizedek. So ask yourself, whom would the Tithe be given to if it was to be still used in the Body of Christ??? We are all preachers of the gospel in some aspect! There is no longer a need for a certain tribe to offer up sacrifices for our sins! So who do we pay Tithes to…each other?

"The Change in the Priesthood"

The author of Hebrews is explaining here that out of the sons of Levi that did receive the office of priesthood had the Commandment to take the Tithes from the Children of Israel. Also, the Children of Israel had the Commandment to give the Tithe (which we have already seen how the priest gave a tenth of a tenth that they received to the High Priest Aaron and his sons for their portion). Nevertheless, the man that was chosen for this particular priesthood was in fact a descendent of Abraham. Melchizedek, however, was not a descendent of Abraham, but he received the Tithes from Abraham. God called all of the High Priests from a certain tribe out of the 12 Tribes of Israel. Levi, which is where the sons of Levi came from, was in the loins of Abraham when Abraham paid Tithes to Melchizedek (verse 10), but there was need of a change. God said in Numbers 18:23,

> *The Levites shall perform the service of the Tabernacle of the Congregation.*

They were chosen along with Aaron and all of his sons to be the priest and High Priest (Num 17). But now, as we have mentioned earlier, there was need for a change, a change in the calling of the High Priest. As we look at Hebrews 7, verses 11 through 18, we can plainly see that the LAW, with its many different commandments, made nothing perfect. Verse 11 says,

> *If therefore perfection were by the Levitical Priesthood (for under IT the people RECEIVED THE LAW) what further need was there that another priest should rise after the order of Melchizedek, and not be called after the order of Aaron? For the priesthood being changed, there is made of necessity a CHANGE ALSO OF THE LAW.*

The LAW had to change because the priesthood changed. No longer is it only one group of people, that based on their genealogy hangs the determining factor of if they can become a priest of God or not. Jesus did not come from the tribe of Levi; he came from the tribe of Judah. Being that the Children of Israel received the LAW under the Levitical Priesthood, they were bound by it and had to carry out every little detail of it in order for them to be righteous in God's eyes. We, being the Children of God through Jesus Christ, also have the LAW that we must follow, which is why Jesus instructed the Disciples to,

> *Go ye therefore, and teach all nations, baptizing them in the name of the Father, and of the Son and of the Holy Ghost: TEACHING THEM TO OBSERVE ALL THINGS WHATSOEVER I HAVE COMMANDED YOU.* Matthew 28:19-20

The Law did not speak of baptism, or casting out demons, or the Gifts of the Holy Spirit! These are things that Jesus commanded us to do! As we have already seen, the things that Jesus commanded the Disciples to do were a combination of the Ten Commandments of the LAW and commandments that he added on to them for the purpose of righteousness. That is why Jesus said,

> *For I say unto you, that except your*
> *righteousness shall exceed the righteousness*
> *of the scribes and Pharisees, ye shall in no*
> *case enter into the kingdom of heaven.*
> Matthew 5:20

After he said these things, he went right into those commandments of old and the things of new that were to be carried out. As I mentioned earlier, I call them the Commandments of Grace because they were given under the Grace we have in Jesus. Jesus called them *"These Least Commandments"*. All of those things that he taught were the New Commandments that you and I are to follow. So from the first thing that Jesus taught until his last parable and commandment before he was ascended to the right hand of the Father, are the things that his followers should adhere to. If we study the New Testament, it will show us exactly what we are to do as Christians and even which commandments of Old were incorporated into the New ones given by Jesus. I know that this is beginning to be clearer to you, so let's continue. Paul summed all of this up for you and I in just two Scriptures: 1 Corinthians 7:19 and John 15:14. Let's look at this portion of the letter that he sent to the Church at Corinth.

> *Circumcision is nothing, and uncircumcision*
> *is nothing, but the keeping of the*
> *commandments of God.* 1st Corinth 7:19

Paul said that being circumcised is not important, but what really mattered was that they keep the Commandments of God. I want to take this moment to make a point here: most people who read this Scripture will take it to mean the Commandments of God that were listed in the LAW of Moses, but it is not. If Paul were talking about the Commandments written under the LAW, then he would have said just that! He would not have stated that circumcision did not matter anymore if he was telling us to continue being obedient to the Law considering that circumcision was a commandment of God during Abraham's time (which was before the LAW) and a commandment that Moses instructed and followed (under the LAW). So you have to ask yourself, what is Paul speaking of when he said to keep the Commandments of God? Well, we can find the answer to this question in the following Scripture,

> *Ye are my friends, if ye do whatsoever **I command you**. Henceforth I call you not servants; for the servant knoweth not what his lord doeth: but I have called you friends; for ALL THINGS THAT I HAVE HEARD OF MY FATHER I HAVE MADE KNOWN UNTO YOU.* John 15:14

This is what Paul was speaking of in 1st Corinth 7:19, the Commandments of Jesus! Oh sure, some might want to argue this fact, but even the best scholar and theologian will agree that these two Scriptures are in fact referencing each other.

It is because of the change in the priesthood, meaning Jesus is our New High Priest, that the Law be changed as well! Again, Jesus changed the Law by his words in Matthew 5, and in all of his different teachings while he was here on Earth. Now, we have our Commandments of God through Jesus Christ that we are to follow because God has established his Son as our High Priest as he said,

> *So also Christ glorified not himself to be made a High Priest; but he that said unto him, Thou art my Son, to day have I begotten thee.* Hebrews 5:5

Paul was not the only disciple of Christ that taught the people about moving away from all of the many different commandments of the LAW. In the book of Acts, chapter

15, verses 5 through 11, Peter is discussing this very subject with a certain sect of the Pharisees. Verse 5 says,

> *But there rose up certain of the sect of the Pharisees which BELIEVED, saying that it was necessary to CIRCUMCISE them, and to COMMAND THEM TO KEEP THE LAW OF MOSES. And the apostles and elders came together for to consider of this matter. And when there had been much DISPUTING, Peter rose up, and said unto them, Men and brethren, ye know how that a good while ago God made choice among us, that the Gentiles by my mouth should hear the word of the gospel, and believe. And God, which knoweth the hearts, bare them witness, giving them the Holy Ghost, even as he did unto us; and made no distinction between them, and us purifying their hearts by faith. NOW THEREFORE WHY TEMPT YE GOD, TO PUT A YOKE UPON THE NECK OF THE DISCIPLES, WHICH NEITHER OUR FATHERS NOR WE WERE ABLE TO BEAR? But we believe that through the grace of the Lord Jesus Christ we shall be saved, even as they.*

I know that was a mouthful, but you really need to get a hold of this. Here are the Disciples, in a land where the LAW was so very much still practiced, trying to teach the people that they no longer had to live according to all of those bits and pieces of the LAW. Peter told them that we should not tempt God to or by placing a yoke around the Disciples' necks that neither their fathers were able to bear! Peter was talking about the yoke of the LAW that Jesus himself had already lifted. Now, if circumcision was addressed in this manner as a yoke of bondage that the Disciples themselves did not want, what makes the Tithe any different? Both the Tithe and Circumcision were practiced by Abraham and later placed in the LAW, so what makes one different from the other? I will tell you what; it's called the Love of Money! Only through the things that Jesus taught us will anyone find their way to God to receive his blessings and not through the works of the LAW.

This is even more evident when we look again at the book of Hebrews in the seventh chapter, verses 18 and 19.

> *For there is verily a SETTING ASIDE OF THE FORMER COMMANDMENTS for the weakness and unprofitable ness thereof. For the Law made nothing perfect, but the bringing in of a better hope did; by the which we draw nigh unto God.*

In this passage of Scripture, we see that the former Commandments were actually set aside and a new hope was brought in. This is the reason why Peter said, *But we believe that through the grace of the Lord Jesus Christ we shall be saved.* He did not say anything about being in trouble for breaking one of the Commandments of the LAW; in fact, he called them a yoke of bondage!

Getting back to the Tithe, we have already stated that some will try and say that since Abraham started the Tithe, it should be a continued practice. But again if that is true, then we should also look at circumcision with the same respect as the Tithe! Now, I know that as Christians God circumcises our hearts, but that is not what we are talking about here. We are talking about the works of the LAW that Abraham did before the LAW was written. Abraham was told to circumcise himself by God before Moses' day, and still circumcision was part of the LAW as was the Tithe; nevertheless, Paul said in Galatians, chapter 6, verse 13,

> *For neither they themselves who are circumcised keep the law; but desire to have you circumcised, that they may glory in your flesh. But God forbid that I should glory, save in the cross of our Lord Jesus Christ, by*

whom the world is crucified unto me, and I unto the world. For in Christ Jesus neither circumcision availeth anything, nor uncircumcision but a new creation.

This again points out to us that the only thing that truly matters is if we have been truly changed from our old self. The things that we did before salvation came are to be set aside, not desired any longer, and from that point on, we are to serve God in a newness of life. I want you to understand that I am not saying the LAW is sin or that we should not read nor believe in the Old Testament. What I'm saying is the same thing that I have been pointing out throughout this entire book. The Ten Commandments was only part of the LAW, and Jesus took those, and throughout his teaching he incorporated them and added to them. The other parts of the Law of Moses that dictate an act or deed that we must do in order to receive from God or to gain righteousness are no longer something that you and I as followers of Christ have to obey. The Tithe was not one of the Ten Commandments, but it was one of the statutes of the Law that had to been done to obtain righteousness. Again, if all of the Law were not carried out then the righteous requirement would not be met and the Curse from the Law came into effect. We are saved from the curse of the Law in Christ Jesus; therefore, those things will not come against you because of the grace given in him.

As we have discussed earlier, the Curse of the Law was that if you did not do everything prescribed in the Law of Moses, then you were cursed with this particular curse. This is why in Malachi, God said, "You are cursed with a curse." I have heard some say that this particular curse mentioned in Malachi means a double curse, but I tell you the truth; that is not what it means. If I were to say to you that you are blessed with a blessing, or even sick with a sickness, what does that mean? I will tell you what it means—it means exactly what it says, that there is a blessing that you are blessed with or a sickness that you are sick with.

Well, the same goes for this curse that is mentioned. Because the people did not follow God's instructions on the Tithe, he said that they had robbed him. So by them breaking the Commandment to Tithe along with all of the other ways that they had went away from God, they were infected with the curse of the Law (SEE DEUTERONOMY 27:26), which put all under a curse for not continuing in all things written under the Law (ALSO SEE GALATIANS 3:10).

I would like to leave you with two things at the end of this chapter: 1) The word of God tells us to study to show ourselves approved unto God and that the Holy Spirit is here to show us all truths. So put these principles to work and watch God reveal his word. 2) As stated in the word of God, I say unto you, *"For if that FIRST covenant had been faultless, THEN should no place have been sought for the SECOND"* (Hebrews 8:7). Therefore, don't try or let anyone else attempt to convince you that the way to receive God's blessings is through the works of the Law. As we can plainly see, our blessings come from our obedience to the Word of God (Jesus) that was made flesh (John 1:14)! It is evident that unless we focus on Jesus, our New Covenant with God the Father, we will lose track of the true way to receive God's blessings! Jesus told us, *I am the way, the truth and the light,* so don't you think that it is safe to say that we should be studying and following the teachings of Jesus and not preaching and practicing the statutes of the Law of Moses? The only way to receive from God whether it is financial, spiritual, physical or emotional blessings is through his only begotten Son, Jesus Christ.

Chapter Four

THE TRUE WAY TO RECEIVE GOD'S BLESSINGS

Throughout this book, we have discussed the Tithe and how the Body of Christ uses it to receive their blessings. Tithing, according to the Scriptures, was a way for the Children of Israel to not only show God how thankful they were for their blessings, but also it was God's way of providing substance for the priest and the sacrifices needed for the atonement of sin (see Leviticus 6:24). All in which established their righteousness, as they were obedient to God's word (see Deut 6:25). The only people that were involved in this cycle were the Children of Israel, Aaron and his sons (the High Priest), and the Levites (the Priest). But all praise belongs to God! Now, under the New Covenant, every single one of us Gentiles (which can mean anyone that is not Jewish or non-Christians among Christians) are now eligible to receive these things and many times more. One of our main problems as the Body of Christ is that we calculate how blessed we are by the amount of money, houses, and other material items obtained in this world. Now, of course, these things can be blessings received, but are they the only way to count our blessings from God? As with a number of other things, we are missing what our Lord was telling us!

Jesus said in Matthew 6-31,

Therefore take no thought saying, what shall we eat? Or, what shall we drink? Or, wherewithal shall we be clothed? (For after all these things do the gentiles seek:) for your heavenly Father knoweth that ye have need of all these things. But seek ye first the kingdom

Anyone who has read and understands this passage of Scripture knows that Jesus was telling us that all things of this world belong to our Father which are in heaven. He will, with no doubt, give us the things that we need in order to survive so that we can carry out the plan of God in our individual lives! But there are also two other things that Jesus was showing us here: (1) We must seek the kingdom of God first and his righteousness in order for us to receive all of these things and more (because God's kingdom has much more than the world can offer), and (2) There is only one way to do this, and that way is through accepting Jesus Christ, the only Son of God, as our personal Savior. After doing so, we will be made righteous in God's eyesight, where in times of old, the Children of Israel would have to do the different parts of the LAW in order to accomplish this same thing.

After we have accepted Jesus as our personal Savior, we must adhere to the things that he commanded us to do and not just disregard what he said by continuing with the commandments of the LAW. I like to refer to the instructions that were given by Christ as the Commandments of Grace because of the undeserving love of the Heavenly Father that he displayed by giving his only Son for our sins. If you ask me, not only did Jesus bear our infirmities and die on the cross for our sins, but he also by doing so earned the right to tell us what we must do in order to keep our reward in Heaven. Remember what Jesus said in Matthew 5:20.

This is one of the reasons why Jesus took the Commandments of the LAW and changed them to the COMMANDMENTS OF GRACE, which are our new set of statutes and ordinances.

"THE LAW OF JESUS"

Let's take a look at what we as Christians (followers of Christ), should be doing in our new life under grace as opposed to that of the LAW.

<u>LAW</u>

1. Thou shalt not murder!

2. Thou shalt not commit adultery!

3. Whosoever shall put away his wife give her a writing of divorcement (for whatever the reason).

4. Thou shalt not swear falsely!

5. Thou shalt love thy neighbor and hate thine enemy!

<u>GRACE</u>

1. Thou shalt not be angry without a cause!

2. Thou shalt not lust (which equals adultery)!

3. Whosoever shall put away his wife except for sexual immorality cause her to commit adultery: and whosoever shall marry her that is divorced committeth adultery!

4. Thou shalt not swear at all!

5. Thou shalt love thy enemies, and bless those that curse you!

Note: *If this is true for all of these Commandments, why is it not true when it comes to this statute?*

6. Thou shalt truly tithe all the increase, that the Lord thy God may bless thee in all the work of thine hand!

6. Give and it shall be given unto you; good measure, pressed down shaken together, and running over, shall men give into your bosom. For with the same measure that ye mete withal it shall be measured to you again.

As you can see, Jesus took the Commandments and expounded on them so that our righteousness would exceed that of the Scribes and Pharisees. However, some of the different statutes of the LAW were not taught by Jesus at all. It is evident that Jesus gave us new statutes that would increase the purpose of the old ones, such as the one concerning the Tithe! As we have seen, when the Children of Israel were being obedient to the tithe (along with all of the other parts of the Law), God would bless them accordingly. On the other hand, Jesus told us that giving would be the determining factor of our receiving from God. As we continue in this chapter, we will examine several instructions that Jesus gave us concerning the things that we are to do in order to receive from God. In the book of Luke, chapter 18, verses 29 through 30, Jesus said,

That you would receive many times more of whatever you forsake for the kingdom of Heaven's sake.

What this means to you and me is that as children of God, when we sacrifice things such as our time, our possessions, our love, or whatever we have that can be used or done away with for the ministering of God's word, those things shall be given back to us many times more. Let's face it, children of God—it is time for the Body of Christ to give more of ourselves. Then, just as the Children of Israel received from God, so shall we. The problem with the Church of today is that we all want to have the blessings of God but not the sacrifices that Jesus spoke of during his many teachings! We are always walking around with our hands open toward heaven saying, "Bless me, bless me, and bless me," not realizing that the blessings come after the responsibility has been accepted. To be totally honest, all we need is more of Jesus in our lives. You see, with our concentration on the wrong things, we will never accomplish that which God has in store for us. Remember what our Lord told us in the book of Matthew, chapter 6, verse 19,

*Lay not up for yourselves treasures upon
earth, for where your treasure is, there will
your heart be also.*

Our hearts should be focused on heaven in every
aspect. Don't get me wrong though because I am not telling
anyone to be so heavenly minded that you are no earthly
good. What I am saying is that there is a dead world out
there lying in darkness, and we need to place all of our
efforts on ministering life and light to them. There is
nothing wrong with having nice things, such as a beautiful
home, or a luxury car, or even a large savings account.
These are all things in the natural that glorify God from a
worldly perspective. But God wants our hearts to be in the
right place so that when these blessings come, we do not lose
focus of our number one priority—getting souls saved!
Besides, how else can you bless someone with an amount of
money if your funds are all dried up?

What if you knew someone that was in desperate
need of a car and you yourself was driving an old beat-up
junker that spent more time in the shop than on the road? Do
you think that they would believe your words of ministry
when you say, *God will supply all your needs according to
his riches in glory*? I don't think so! It all boils down to the
fact that God wants us to walk in his blessings and to have
nice things, but God never intended for the things to have us!
This is where the problem comes in; most people don't even
think about God until they need something. As long as
everything is all right, they simply place God on a shelf until
the next time they run into trouble. This is not the Biblical
way to follow Christ!

Following Christ means to first take up our cross
daily by walking in his examples and having a personal
relationship with him as our Lord and Savior. I am not
telling people to go out and crucify themselves, but what I
mean by taking up our cross daily does equal crucifying our
flesh by denying it the sinful desires. Once we know Jesus, I

mean truly know him, then we begin to recognize what our time on this earth is supposed to be used for. We were not placed here to simply get saved and wander around in a state of entry-level consciousness as babes in Christ. No, we all have a plan and a purpose in life that lines up with God's perfect will! What we have to do is seek him for our individual plan, study God's word (which is Jesus in the flesh), trust in him, obey him, and worship his Holy name! But most Christians will not seek the Lord, nor study his word. It's like the author said in Hebrews 5:12,

> *For when for the time ye ought to be teachers,*
> *ye have need that one teach you again which*
> *be the first principles of the oracles of God;*
> *and are become such as have need of milk,*
> *and not of strong meat.*

If we don't study, then we will not trust him nor obey him because we don't know his promises and we don't know what he has told us to do! As far as worshiping him, most think that an occasional prayer and a visit to their church on Sunday, or Saturday, are sufficient. Well, if you are one of those "Occasional Christians" mentioned here, then just pick up your Bible sometimes and read the book of Psalms. See how David worshiped God, and maybe this will break some of those Religious Traditions of Men that have been wedged in your mind and spirit. Now, I am a true believer in the power of worship! I mean there is something very special and powerful in the worshiping of our Lord! But again, in order to worship him, you must first know him. I suppose that you are asking, "What does this have to do with the true way to receive God's blessings?" Well, it has everything to do with it—that's what! Knowing Jesus is the beginning of our relationship with God the Father! Jesus said,

> *I am the way, the truth, and the light; no one*
> *comes to the Father (God) except by me.*

So if anyone were to receive anything from God, then one would have to believe and receive God's plan for salvation, which we know is that which Jesus did at Calvary. I say this because so many Christians do not even know their Savior the way that he intended for us to know him. All of the teachings, parables, commandments, and the ultimate sacrifice that Jesus demonstrated are to be, our focal points as Christians! If we (Christians) would study and practice the things instructed to us by Jesus, then the blessings would not be something that we would have to constantly ask for or even look for! Not only would we not have to look for them, but also we definitely would not have to go back to the commandments of the Law to try and receive our blessings! Jesus made our instructions quite simple and plain for us to receive our blessings. Looking again at the book of Matthew 6:33, a well-known Scripture, we can break down what Jesus tells us to do.

> *Seek the Kingdom of Heaven and its righteousness first and all of these things shall be added unto you.*

But what were *These Things* that we as believers were to receive and what is the *Righteousness* of the Kingdom? Well, we know that the kingdom of Heaven is basically the Kingdom of God or God's Kingdom. The righteousness spoken of here is Jesus himself. So Jesus was telling us that we must gain God's righteousness by receiving him and therefore ultimately gaining entrance into God's Kingdom! Romans 3:19-22 confirms this by saying,

> *But now the righteousness of God apart from the Law is revealed, being witnessed by the Law and the Prophets, even the righteousness of God, through faith in Jesus Christ, to all and on all who believe.*

So what were the things that would be added unto us after finding God's righteousness in Jesus? We simply need to look at the verses, in Matthew 6 for the answer. In verses 25-32, we see that as followers of Christ, we are commanded to not worry about our life, food, drink, or clothing. Some may not look at *These Things* as blessings, but I certainly do! There are so many people in the world that do not have *These Things,* while we take them for granted. These are the basic necessities of life that God has promised for those who believe in his Son! So if we believe, then what should we be doing on a daily basis to receive "These Things" along with the other blessings that we will discuss?

Surely worrying is not something that is required of us as Christians, but don't we commit this awful act of sin in our faith department all of the time? God provides *These Things* so that we can focus on our lifestyles and our calling in Christ. Does God's word give us provisions for our lifestyles? Of course it does! Let's take a look at how we, as believers, should conduct ourselves in order to receive. In Matthew 5-20, Jesus told us,

> *Unless your righteousness exceeds the righteousness of the Scribes and Pharisees, you will by no means enter the Kingdom of Heaven.* Our Lord also told us in verse 19 that, *Whoever therefore breaks one of the least of these commandments, and teach men so, shall be called least in the Kingdom of Heaven; but whoever does and teaches them, he shall be called great in the Kingdom of Heaven (or God's Kingdom).*

Immediately after Jesus said this he began to list the commandments of old and change them to what he called *"Least of these Commandments"*. Just take a moment to look at them again to allow it to sink in. So this simply means that as Christians we are commanded by the Son of the Living God to not only keep his commandments but also to not carry ourselves as the Scribes and Pharisees did. If you are again asking, "What does this have to do with receiving from God?" Well, this is our Savior telling his followers how to live their lives, correct? Then, if we obey him by keeping his commandments, then we are his, and he abides in us.

Therefore, we have the capabilities to ask what we desire and it shall be done for us as pointed out to us in John 15:5. Is this not receiving a blessing? Of course it is! In Matthew 6, Jesus points out that we are not to do our charitable deeds before men. He said,

> *That your charitable deed may be in secret;*
> *and your Father who sees in secret will*
> *himself reward you openly.*

Reward? Is that not a blessing? In verse 5, Jesus tells us to pray but not out loud in the public places to be seen of men, but if we pray in our closet or secret place, he said,

> *Your Father who sees in secret will reward*
> *you openly.*

Reward? Is that another blessing? Now, this next set of words is so very clear but seldom practiced. Jesus said in verse 7,

> *And when you pray do not heap up empty*
> *phrases as the Gentiles do; for they think that*
> *they will be heard for their many words. Do*
> *not be like them, for your Father knows what*
> *you need before you ask him.*

God already knows what's in our hearts and what we need. This is why Jesus said that all of *These Things* shall be added unto us. This is also why he gave us the prayer to say in verse 9. All of this points to us as being followers that obey and how we will receive in return. In verse 14 Jesus said that we must forgive others so that we can be forgiven. In verse 16 he talks about when we fast and how not to show ourselves to the world as sad because of our fast. If we do this in secret, then once again, God will reward us openly. Will you look at that—another blessing!

So we receive our blessings, as followers of Christ, by obeying what Jesus taught us to do who is the Righteousness of God! Not by attempting to obtain our own righteousness in the same manner as those who lived and followed the Law of Moses! Let's continue to look at the commandments given to us by Jesus, and then we will take a look at the bad examples found in the life-styles of the Scribes and Pharisees.

"THESE LEAST COMMANDMENTS"

Now, in the beginning of this chapter, we looked at the teachings of Jesus in comparison to the Law of Moses. We saw how in Matthew 5:21 that Jesus took some of the Ten Commandments and expounded on them. We see our new commandments of grace, which Jesus called, *These Least Commandments*. Now, I know that most Christians don't even practice the Ten Commandments let alone *These Least Commandments,* but it is time that we focus our minds on the things that Jesus commanded us to do. Again, Jesus did not destroy the Law; he fulfilled it, which means that he is the manifestation of the things, which the Prophets spoke of, and that he has fulfilled the righteousness requirement of the Law that no man could do! To me, Jesus made these *Least Commandments* much more strict so that our righteousness would indeed exceed that of the Scribes and Pharisees. Take, for example, the Law of Adultery. Under the Law, you had to have some type of physical contact in order to commit Adultery. But Jesus said,

> *That whosoever looketh on a woman to lust after her hath committed adultery with her already in his heart.* Matthew 5:28

Now, I have heard so many men say, "I have not done anything wrong by looking at another woman!" I have even heard some go as far to say, "Hey, I might be on a diet, but I can still look at the menu!" But according to the word of God (Jesus Christ), this man has already had a sexual experience with the woman through his lustful eye.

Getting back to God's blessings, as mentioned earlier, so many Christians think that the only way to measure blessings is in a monetary value. But is this true according to the word of God (Jesus)? The answer is NO! Look at Matthew 5, verses 3-11.

Blessed are the Meek, Blessed are those who hunger and thirst for righteousness, Blessed are the merciful, Blessed are the pure in heart, Blessed are the peacemakers, Blessed are those who are persecuted for righteousness sake, Blessed are you when people speak evil against you and persecute you.

Now, I don't know about you, but that seems to be a Whole Lot of Blessings to me! How many times did Jesus use the word *Blessed* in these verses? Why have we overlooked these in our teachings at church? I will tell you why; because if you noticed, these blessings did not come from you opening your wallet/purse; they came from the conditions of your heart. I will take you even deeper than that; remember when Moses, Aaron, and the 12 sons of Israel were standing on the mountains issuing out the Blessings and Curses over the Children of Israel? Jesus is doing the exact same thing here during his sermon on the mountain. But what happened to the Curses? Why didn't Jesus proclaim the Curse from the Law? I will tell you why; Jesus redeemed us from that curse, and as he said in verse 17,

I am not come to destroy, but to fulfill.

We can see that Jesus wanted us to believe in him, follow his *Least Commandments* and to achieve a greater righteousness than that of the Scribes and Pharisees. In return, our blessings would include necessities in life, having the ability to ask God for things, God knowing and giving us things, inheriting things such as the earth and heaven, and to receive the other things mentioned in these passages of

Scripture. We all know that it takes money to accomplish things in life, but wouldn't that make money a necessity as well? Of course it is, and whether we need it for everyday life or to accomplish that which we are called by God to do, God will provide for us as he has promised!

"Scribes and Pharisees"

A Scribe was a person, learned in the Jewish Law, who made handwritten copies of the Torah, which were the collection of Jewish religious literature. The Pharisees were the religious Jewish members of Jesus' time, as well as before, who not only carefully observed the written Law but also accepted the oral or traditional law of religious practices. They were highly esteemed because they held positions of authority within the religious community by sitting in Moses' seat. Many times they would look down upon and condemn people for committing sin and breaking the Law of Moses when they themselves would do the same. Jesus told us that if we did not exceed their righteousness, then we would not see the Kingdom of God!

This is an allegory; Moses was the chosen leader of the Children of Israel that lead them out of Egypt. But Moses did not lead the Children of Israel into the promised land because of his disobedient act with the water of Mer'-i-bah (See Num 20:9-12/27:12-18/Deut 34:4). Now Jesus said that the Scribes and Pharisees sit in Moses Seat and that if we do not obtain a greater state of righteousness then they, we would not enter into the Kingdom of God. Can you see the correlation? Not taking anything from Moses, but here we can see how he did not enter into the Promised Land due to his disobedience to God's commandment. Under the Law, the righteousness requirement could only be met if they did all; but Moses missed the mark. The Scribes and Pharisees were sitting in Moses seat of authority over the Children of Israel and just as Moses did, they were missing the mark.

This is why Jesus told us that if our righteousness will not exceed theirs, then we, just as Moses did not enter the promised land and the Scribes and Pharisees will not enter into the Kingdom of God, neither shall we!

So let's take a look at some of their ways. In Matthew 23, Jesus discusses a long list of the things in which he did not want his followers to do. He said that the Scribes and Pharisees would, *Say, and do not do.* Jesus does not want us to be hypocrites as these religious people were. Jesus was telling us to be a people of action that lined up with our words. He wants us to not only speak the things of God, but to do them as well. He tells of how they will not help others with their burdens, even if they were the cause of it. Did you ever have someone cause you some problems and they would not even say 'I am sorry' or attempt to help you to fix the problem that they caused?

Jesus talked about how they do their works out in the open just to be seen by men. Now, would this be that sister who always wants to be in the spotlight at church but will curse you out if you cross her the wrong way? Jesus tells of how they love to be seen in the public places and sitting in the best seats. What about that person who sits in the same seat at church all of the time (and you better not sit there)? We have all seen these examples in different proportions, but are we the ones posing in these positions instead of someone else? All of these examples point to one thing—*Pride*! Psalms 10:4 reads,

> *The wicked, through the pride of his countenance (or the way one holds oneself), will not seek after God: God is not in all his thoughts.*

You see, Pride is what causes us to look down upon others. Pride is what makes us think that we are better than others. It was pride that caused the Scribes and Pharisees to act or carry themselves in the manner that caused Jesus to look at them in this way. Do we want God looking at us this way? Then we better learn the ways of a humble man and do it fast! In Matthew 23:12, Jesus told us,

> *And whosoever shall exalt himself shall be abased; and he that shall humble himself shall be exalted.*

In the previous verses, Jesus is describing how these same Scribes and Pharisees just love to be called by their title of *Rabbi* or *Father (verses 8-9)*. Now, this is what's very disturbing to me. I have heard people say, "Oh Bishop So-and-So is my Spiritual Father." What??? I mean they have taken this Scripture and ripped it out of the Word of God! Come on now, Saints if God is our Father and his Holy Spirit is our comforter, then how can we even possibly believe that a man is our Spiritual Father? We have got to really wake up! Jesus specifically said, *"Call No Man Father."* How much more clear can the Scriptures be? I don't even refer to my earthly dad as Father for this exact same reason. He is Dad, or Daddy, or even Pop, if you will, but our Father is in Heaven. Hey, don't get mad at me because I did not say it—Jesus did! This is why he told us, *When you pray, pray our Father who are in Heaven.*

Now, concerning the blessings of God in lieu of the Tithe, I have heard several pastors say that Matthew 23:23 proves that Jesus was telling the people to Tithe, and they use this as one of the Scriptures to justify it. Well, this is the furthest thing from the truth, and we have looked at this Scripture in previous chapters. "Oh but Brother Coman, in Matthew 23:23, Jesus convicted the Scribes about not doing what the LAW said about the Tithe." You are exactly right!

Let's take a look at what Jesus really said.

> *Woe unto you, Scribes and Pharisees, HYPOCRITES! For ye pay Tithe of mint and anise and cumin and have neglected the weightier matters of the LAW, Justice, mercy,*

and faith: these ought ye to have done, and
not to leave the other undone.

You see, Jesus was making a point about the Scribes being hypocrites for doing only parts of the LAW and not the whole thing. If anyone is trying to justify Tithing based on this Scripture, then that person is telling you and me that we should be doing all of the LAW. Isn't that what Jesus was pointing out here—hypocrisy? One of the parallel Scriptures to this one is over in Luke. Jesus is telling a parable of two men that were in the temple praying. One man was a Pharisee and the other a tax collector. Now, in Jesus' day, if you were a tax collector, you were not a very popular person. So in this parable, Jesus describes how the two men stood there praying to God. Luke 18:11 reads,

> *The Pharisee stood and prayed thus with himself, God, I thank thee, that I am not as other men are, extortioners, unjust, adulterers, or even as this tax collector. I fast twice in the week; I give Tithes of all that I possess. And the Tax Collector standing afar off, would not lift up so much as his eyes unto heaven, but beat upon his breast, saying God be merciful to me a sinner. I tell you, this man went down to his house justified rather than the other.*

Again, Jesus was pointing out here that being a humble sinner is more important than being a boastful hypocrite! Besides, during this particular time that Jesus came on the scene, the LAW was still in full effect; therefore, if someone was not doing everything that was established in the LAW, and/or condemning others, they were considered to be hypocrites. Think about this, if Jesus was telling the Scribes and Pharisees that they were hypocrites because they paid tithe and did not do the other parts of the LAW, how much more of a hypocrite are those that are no longer under the LAW that continue to tithe and do not practice the many different other works of the LAW?

If I told my wife that I think she should spend more time praying, and I myself would go for days and days without praying, then I would fall under the same category as the Scribes and the Pharisees, because I'm teaching men to do something that I don't do myself. This passage of Scripture is sometimes taken out of context in that people want to say that Jesus was telling us to tithe, when you and I both can plainly see that he was only using it to point out their hypocrisy; as you continue to read, you can see it even more. Back over in Matthew 23, Jesus told the Disciples,

> *The Scribes and the Pharisees sit on Moses'*
> *seat; so practice and observe whatever they*
> *tell you, but not what they do.*

"Aha! I told you, Brother Coman, that we are supposed to Tithe because right here Jesus told the Disciples to obey the leaders of their day!" Think about it, Children of God, you must remember that while Jesus walked the earth the Law of Moses and all of its commandments and statutes (even blood sacrifices) were still being practiced by the Children of Israel. So are we to continue with blood sacrifices as well? God forbid! Jesus had not totally fulfilled the Law until he would ascend to the right hand of the Father! Therefore, all of the practices of the Law were still being accomplished. Jesus knew that all righteousness had to be adhered to in order for his task to be completed on the cross. This is even evident when John the Baptist was in the wilderness baptizing people. Jesus came to him to be baptized, but John said that Jesus should baptize him instead. Jesus told John that this must be done in order for all righteousness to be fulfilled. Jesus also knew that the Disciples were not ready to stand up against the religious system of that day and they would not be ready until God endowed them with power by the comforter.

This is why he told them in Acts 1:7-8,

> *He said to them, "It is not for you to know
> times or seasons which the Father has fixed
> by his own authority. But you shall receive
> power when the Holy Spirit has come upon
> you and you shall be "MY" witnesses in
> Jerusalem and in all Judea and Samaria and
> to the end of the earth.*

Jesus knew that the time for the Disciples to stand boldly and proclaim the New covenant had not come. So naturally, the Disciples had to obey the current leadership that existed, the Scribes and Pharisees but he told them not to do as they did; proving he was only pointing out their hypocrisy. This, coupled with the fact that Jesus had to bear the hatred and jealousy of the Scribes and Pharisees alone, was the reason for him telling them to obey their words. This Scripture is not to be used as justification for the Tithe because all of the Law was being practiced during this time.

Think about it, Jesus was sending his Disciples into all of Jerusalem and eventually the world. In Jerusalem the Law of Moses was being followed (or shall I say attempted to be followed) by every Jewish person and others that lived there. These same people did not accept Jesus and even called him a blasphemer! Why? Because his teachings did not follow their way of interpreting the Law! So how much more would the Scribes and Pharisees not have believed nor listened to the Disciples?

"Oh Ye of Little Faith"

The issue and point here is focusing on the "Great Commission" in which each and every member of the Body of Christ are called to do. This is clearly pointed out in the 28th chapter of Matthew, when Jesus commissioned each and every believer to do something; he said, *Go ye therefore, and teach all nations.* This is not to say that every member of the Body of Christ is called to be an evangelist, but it is sending out a message to us all. The message is plain and simple: whatever city or town or neighborhood we encounter and or live in is indeed that nation he spoke of to reach with the Gospel of Jesus Christ. Okay, so you are not outgoing enough to knock on your neighbor's door, but what about that coworker that is less than twenty feet from you whom you know is lost? Are you ashamed of the gospel? Jesus said in Mark 8:38,

> *Whosoever therefore shall be ashamed of me*
> *and of my words in this adulterous and sinful*
> *generation; of him also shall the Son of man*
> *be ashamed, when he cometh in the glory of*
> *his Father with the holy angels.*

So it is mandated that we share the gospel regardless of our calling. For some, it is simply an issue of faith! In Matthew 6:30, Jesus said,

> *Wherefore if God so clothe the grass of the*
> *field, which today is, and tomorrow is cast*
> *into the oven, shall he not much more clothe*
> *you, O YE OF LITTLE FAITH?*

Jesus is simply saying that our needs, our wants, and the desires of our hearts are already known of God; all we need to do is to have faith in him. So many times we as Christians fill the necessity to assist God by making up religious rules, and adding Scriptures from the Old and New Testament to make it all sound spiritual. When in all actuality, we can only receive our blessings from God through our Faith in his Son, Jesus, not through the works of the LAW! When Jesus said, *Therefore take no thought*, and then he said, *For your heavenly Father knoweth that ye have need of all these things,* again, he was talking about necessities!

I can't count how many times I have heard great preachers of the gospel, standing on national television, displaying their unbelief in this very passage of Scripture by literally begging other members of the Body of Christ to send and support their ministry. Not only do they rely on the people, but also they even give the supporters the glory by saying, "This ministry cannot continue without your financial support." Where is the faith in God? It is God that gives man the desire to give things to the different ministries; so where is your faith, oh man of God? Jesus has already told us that God already knew of the things in which we need to survive with, especially if we are called by him to accomplish a mission. It's all right to give people the opportunity to sow a seed into your ministry and even to give honor to whom honor is due (Romans 13:7), but please don't take God's glory in the process!

So we are not to worry about our needs in the ministry, especially if we are called of God. The word of God tells us that our needs can be taken care of through our service in the preaching of the gospel!

Paul wrote in 1 Corinthians 9:7,

Who serves as a soldier at his own expense?
Who plants a vineyard without eating any of
its fruit? Who tends a flock without getting
some of the milk?

So it is understood that individuals within the ministry can reap benefits from the ministry, but we are not to abuse this privilege. Paul confirms this in verse 12.

Nevertheless, we have not made use of this
right, but we endure anything rather than
place an obstacle in the way of the gospel of
Christ.

This *obstacle* that Paul mentioned here is that feeling a person gets when they hear a minister asking for money. At that moment, most people will totally forget what the message is and start to focus on a man that is asking them for money. Paul was pointing this out to illustrate that it is okay to receive money from the ministry for personal use but he, along with others, would not do it, so that no one could say that their ministry was simply a way to get money from the people. Paul knew the repercussions of this act of asking for money and how it would cause an obstacle in the minds of the people from receiving the good news of Christ Jesus.

Some will say that it was Paul's choice to not receive substance from his works in the gospel, and they would be absolutely correct. But again, it is the condition of our hearts that God looks at! God is going to provide for us, and he does provide for us through the ministry, but it is our responsibility to keep things in the correct perspective! So just as Paul said in verse 16,

> *For necessity is laid upon me,* verse 18, *What then is my reward? Just this: that in my preaching I may make the gospel free of charge, not making full use of my right in the gospel.*

It is a minister's full right to secure provisions by way of the gospel, but again, it is their responsibility to control the greed that can so easily be associated with it! Also, this particular passage of Scripture does not justify Tithing. In verse 13 Paul was using the illustration of how the Priests that worked in the temple got their food from their work in the temple and he was comparing that process to how the ministers of the gospel should get their living by the gospel. He did not say that the ministers of the gospel are to use the Tithe! Think about it—if he was saying that the ministers of the gospel are to use the Tithe but that he chose not to, would that not cause Paul to sin considering it was a commandment to the Levites to receive the Tithe?

Paul understood that the Tithe was meant for the Priests in the temple and not for the ministers of the gospel. Why else would he distinguish between the two in his comparison? He could have easily said for the ministers of the gospel to use the Tithe from the Temple for their substance. He did not because he knew that along with the change in the priesthood came a change in the source (the Tithe vs. the Ministry of Giving).

Money should never be a motivational factor to help those in need. It is the love and compassion of Christ that should compel us. Remember what the Disciples said in Acts, 3:6 to the lame man in the temple who asked for money,

> *Then Peter said, Silver and gold have I none;*
> *but such as I have give I thee: In the name of*
> *Jesus Christ of Nazareth rise up and walk.*

Peter gave to this man from his love and compassion, not from his wallet; neither did he want anything from this lame man for the gift. We think that it's all about money in today's ministry. We use the Tithe as a means to threaten the Body of Christ so that our pockets are fat and we don't have to worry about how the lights at the church are going to stay on! That is not the way; it only takes prayer and faith in God to get the ball rolling! In 2nd Corinthians, chapter 5, verse 7, Paul tells us that we are to walk by faith and not by sight! If we truly had faith in God, we would not be falling apart when things get a little rough. Proverbs 3:5 says,

> *Trust in the Lord with all thine heart; and*
> *lean not unto thine own understanding. In all*
> *thy ways acknowledge him and he shall*
> *MAKE SMOOTH THY PATHS.*

If God has this in his word, then shouldn't we be living by it? Let's face it—when God has something planned for us to do, nothing can stand in the way—except for us! Some of our paths have giant boulders in them, and the only way to remove them is by having faith and trusting in God for whatever it is that we need. More than likely, these boulders are there because of our unbelief and God is trying to make us aware of them so that we can "Let go and let God." If the boulders that are in our paths just happen to be financial boulders, then making threats to the Body of Christ is not the answer. Instead, we should be *"Acknowledging God in all of our ways"* so that he gets the glory, and then our missions in life will be successful.

How many times have you heard this statement made, "If you do not Tithe, then you are under a curse from God, but you can still go to heaven"? This is the furthest thing from the truth that I have ever heard. There is no such thing as being disobedient and obedient at the same time. If you are being disobedient to God's word, then you are sinning, and we all know that living in sin will stop you from entering into the pearly gates. True enough in Malachi 3:9, God said by way of the prophet, *"Ye are cursed with a curse"*, but are we still being justified under the works of the LAW or are we under the Grace given in our Lord and Savior Jesus Christ? This question is clearly answered by Paul in Galatians 5:1-8. Paul said,

> *Whosoever of you are justified by the LAW;*
> *ye are fallen from grace.* Galatians 5:4

This is the only way that a born-again believer can possibly be under a curse—by stepping out of that which has saved us and back into that which condemned us.

"But I Have Been Blessed by My Tithing"

Now, you may ask the question, "How could I have been receiving my blessings based on my Tithing, if Tithing is not the true way to receive from God?" Well, ask yourself this, "Have I truly received a blessing that I did not have room enough to receive?" That is what the Scripture in Malachi promised! Or have you, just like everyone else, received a **measure** of what you have placed into the kingdom? Understand, we are under Grace and should Give;

112

Tithing was a commandment of the Law, written for those under the Law as seen in Romans,

> *Whatever the law says it speaks to those who are under the law.* (See Romans 3:19.)

Getting back to Galatians, Paul was pointing out to us that no man is justified or declared righteous by the LAW. Therefore, Christ fulfilled the LAW and made a way for you and me to become righteous before God through him. The final point that Paul was making here is that there is no way you nor I could be under a curse, especially one from the LAW, because Christ has not only redeemed us from the curse, but in fact he has even become a curse for us on the cross. Galatians 3:13 reads,

> *Christ hath redeemed us from the curse of the law, being made a curse for us: for it is written, Cursed is every one that hangeth on a tree.*

Here is the answer to the question mentioned earlier, "How could I have been receiving my blessings based on my Tithing if Tithing is not the way for us to receive?" You and I are under grace, and our guidance is clear; Give and it shall be given unto you! It does not matter what you have called or classified your giving as; it is still an amount of money that you have sown into the kingdom! You can call it your Tithe, or an Offering, or a Gift, but because you are a child of God, giving money for the purpose of spreading the Gospel is the reason why you have received in return. You see, Christ has even become this curse that Paul is talking about that people are under for only doing part of the LAW. Like I mentioned before, if you or I stepped out of the will of God, then of course anything could happen to us. But what we are addressing here is that you are still a born-again believer who gives money every so often and calls it the Tithe.

You are not in this category of people who believe that instead of excepting Jesus they can just do the different parts of the LAW and be accepted by God. In their case if they were to only do parts of the LAW and not all of it, then they would be under this curse spoken of in the book of Malachi. All of us, at times, do things that without God's Fatherly love would be detrimental. But because of Christ, we can be forgiven for our mistakes and continue in our walk with God. We being followers of Christ should not follow in the footsteps of those that try to receive from God by doing parts of the LAW, such as the Tithe, but stick to that which Jesus has taught us. Even the Children of Israel could not keep all of the LAW, so why should we try to emulate their works?

Paul himself has pointed out that the blood of Christ is sufficient to redeem us from the curse. Jesus has already done this once; he is not going to go back to the cross just because we decide that we should return to the works of the LAW. To make it plain and simple, by returning to the individual works of the LAW, we are just spinning our wheels! The financial blessings that you have received are not because of your faithfulness to the works of the LAW, but for the simple fact that you are a child of God and that he has already told us in his Word that he would supply our every need! Remember, God honors any vow that we make to him. So it is not the Tithe working in your life, but it is the simple fact that because you are giving money, as a vow to God, for what you believe is the work of the kingdom that God is blessing you. If you think that you are being blessed now, I wonder how you will react when you start receiving from God because of your newly found freedom in giving and not being bound to the ten percent rule of the Tithe!

God has always wanted his people to give and help others. This is evident in the purpose of the "Three Year Tithe" which we will look at again, later on in this chapter. For now, remember what you have learned this far and do as Paul told the Galatians in chapter 5:1,

*Stand fast therefore in the liberty wherewith
Christ hath made us free, and be not
entangled again with the yoke of bondage.*

This yoke of bondage spoken of by Paul and the other Apostles, is in fact the works of the Law (Acts 15:1-11). God's Grace is truly sufficient!

Let's continue to look at what Jesus taught us to do to receive. Now, I hope that no one misunderstands what I am saying to mean that we as the Body of Christ do not need money and should not develop plans and strategies to get God's word out to the world. What I am saying is, as the Body of Christ, we should focus on getting the word out (the Gospel), and let God take care of the increase portion. In Matthew 7:7-11, Jesus said,

*Ask and it shall be given you; for everyone
that asketh, receiveth.*

In James 4:2, the Word says,

Yet ye have not because you ask not.

Many of us struggle through life barely making it from payday to payday. (Trust me, I have been there.) What kind of example are we setting for the world to follow? Jesus said,

*Ye are the light of the world, let it shine
before men that they may see your good
works, and glorify your Father which is in
heaven.*

Jesus was not talking about our wealth here but our actions and demonstration of God's love to our fellow man. The problem is when the church is in the same position as the world; who can tell were the light is coming from or if it is even shining? Who wants to be a shining example for others when they are so depressed because of bills on top of bills? Besides all of that, do we really think for one moment that being in poverty glorifies God the Father? If we truly think so, then we need to take another looooong look! We have to rise above our situations so that regardless of what we are going through, our faith stands firm as a shining example until the manifestation of our prayers are seen. We must continue to be patient and stay focused on our mission as soldiers of the Most High—God!

Some think that the Tithe is the only way that the church can get and stay out of debt while helping others to do the same. Well, this is very true! The church could accomplish being debt free by their members paying the Tithe (ten percent of an individuals' income), but this can also be accomplished with any substantial amount of money coming in on a steady basis! But there is something wrong with the concept of using the Tithe to do this, as we have discussed in detail. The Tithe is not the way, especially if we are going to use it as a threat. What we need to do is to stop using a curse from the law to place fear in people simply because the leadership does not have enough faith in God for their increase.

Most pastors cannot even phantom a way to survive without the Tithe. But honestly, if the first church, in the book of Acts, did it then we can as well. If the church leadership would just stop being so secretive about the financial needs of their churches then the members would give accordingly. Besides, I am sure that the money needed is being used for the work of spreading the gospel,,,,,right? Oh but I can just hear in my spirit the words of some, "Aw brother Coman, you have apparently never had a church of your own with all of the problems that are associated with the members"! Well I say to those pastors that you probably need to take a close look at your mission statement and compare it to the Word of God. Maybe, just maybe, you need to stop in the middle of your all too familiar "Service", tell everyone with a loud voice to "Follow Me", and head out into that lost neighborhood that is right outside your church door! With your members focused on the "True" mission of the Body of Christ, they will not have time for all of that worldly non-sense! Hasn't it been said that an idol mind is the Devil's playground? Simply put, we need to allow the Body of Christ to know and understand what our individual church plans consist of, so the people will be willing to give money, or their time, or any other means of support.

Some try to entangle our situation of today with that of the first church. This is idiotic because in the first church the people would sell possessions and bring the money to place it at the feet of the Disciples. Afterwards the Disciples would distribute the money out to whoever needed it. If the Tithe was the way to finance the first church's mission, then why didn't the Disciples simply tell the people to Tithe? The reason they didn't is crystal clear—the Tithe was a totally different provision. It was not meant for the same purpose as the bringing in of money to lie down at the Disciples' feet.

Does this sound familiar to you, *If you do not Tithe, you cannot and will not receive your blessings from God?* After this, there is always the quoting of Malachi 3:10.

> *God said bring ye all the Tithes into the storehouse, that there may be meat in mine house, and prove me now herewith, saith the Lord of hosts, if I will not open you the windows of heaven, and pour you out a blessing that there shall not be room enough to receive it.*

Now, there is no doubt that this is the written word of God, but as we have already examined in the previous chapters, the Tithe was only for a certain group of people, which means that the promise made here was also for that select few. On the other hand, through Jesus Christ, we have a new plan to receive; he told us that if we would just GIVE, then it would be given unto us with the same measure that we mete WITHAL it shall be measured to us again!

This means that if you give, let's say, love to someone who is lonely, then I guarantee you yourself will never be lonely. What if you needed a certain thing and there was a person who had an abundance of that very thing—wouldn't you want that person to help you? Well, that is exactly what God expects us as his children to do! He has already said in his word that there are certain things that his children would never go without, such as food, clothing, water, protection, so there is no excuse for Christians to be selfish and not share and help others. Of course the fact that God is going to provide for us should not be our reason to help others. However, it should be because we have the love of Christ dwelling in and flowing out of us. As you can see, the principles have changed since Christ has become our High Priest. Paul said in 2 Corinthians 3:6,

> *The letter Killeth, but the spirit giveth life, that the ministry of death, written and engraved in STONE (the LAW) was glorious, so that the children of Israel could not steadily behold the face of Moses for the glory of his countenance; which glory was passing away: how shall not the ministry of the Spirit be more glorious.*

It is the New Covenant that is the basis of our ministry. Paul was showing us how the LAW was so glorious that when Moses came down from the mountain his face shown with the Glory of God, but it was not something that would continue; that is why he said that it was passing away, but now we have the ministry of the spirit, which is far more glorious than that of the LAW. So why are we still trying to justify ourselves by the provisions of the LAW? Some use this excuse all of the time, "Well, God said, he is the same yesterday, today, and forever." Amen brother, this is exactly what Jesus said, but does this mean that God cannot change his mind sometime? That's right; he has in the past, and he will in the future; the choice is ours. Just take a look at the Old Testament and how many times God was going to smite someone, but because there was an intervention by one of the saints, God had mercy. Not only is it possible for God to change the out-come of someone or a situation but there is a totally different way in which God deals with man under his New Covenant. If you don't believe that things are different between the overall spirit of the New Covenant vs. the Old Covenant, just take a look at what Jesus said in Luke 9:56.

> *And when his disciples James and John saw this, they said, Lord, wilt thou that we command fire to come down from heaven, and consume them, even as Elias did? But he (Jesus) turned, and rebuked them, and said, Ye know not what manner of spirit ye are of.*

This is unquestionable proof that the change from the Old Covenant to the New Covenant is not only a new agreement between man and God, but even we are governed by a different spirit of God than those of old. What? Yeah that's right—I said it and I stand on it as well. Why do you think the above scripture shows a distinction between the actions of Elias, which lived in the Old Testament under the Law vs. the actions of Jesus. Not to mention the shear fact that Jesus said, *"Ye know not what manner of spirit ye are of"*. Remember, God has 7 spirits, which in Revelation are represented by the 7 candles. Don't tell me our God is not powerful enough to do this—'cause he is! Remember when Ezekiel saw the Cherub of God? He described it as a creature with four sides, and each side had four faces on it. Now, when Moses was on the mountain, he saw a burning bush and God's voice was coming from the midst, and while the spirit of God led them in the wilderness, it was a Cloud by day and a pillar of Fire by night. But when Jesus came up from the water during his baptism, it was a dove that landed on him, and the Bible said,

> *And Jesus, when he was baptized, went up straightway out of the water: and, lo, the heavens were opened unto him, and he saw*

These are all manifestations of God's spirit! Now, I am only saying this because it is important that we understand the nature of God's spirit that we are under being followers of Christ. Jesus came to bring life, peace, and joy, which are all symbolic of a dove. Whereas the spirit, that Ezekiel saw was not like this one, and neither was the ones that Moses experienced. Therefore, knowing these Scriptures and coupled with the words of Jesus, we can safely say that there is a major difference!

The Tithe as we have already seen was not meant for any of the reasons that the church of today uses it for, and this alone is enough proof that the Tithe is being misused. One way that the Tithe is being misused is that it is used to threaten as mentioned earlier! Listen to me, child of God, it is unquestionable that the Tithe is no longer a commandment that we must follow in order to receive blessings and to stay away from the curses; however, the commandment to give is what every born-again Christian should be practicing. We all know that God loves a cheerful giver, and therefore, giving is something that we should enjoy doing. Not only are we helping others, but we are also being obedient to God's word and he will honor that just as he always did.

The members of the five-fold ministry should not have to use the Tithe or any other persuasion in order to get us to give back to God's kingdom; we should be willing to do it on our own! God did not force us to accept his Son as our Savior, and he is not going to force us to obey his word neither! On that same note, if the five-fold ministry would repent from misusing the Tithe and proclaiming a curse over the people of God that Jesus himself became for us, then we could continue in the things of God where the Disciples left off. For this reason, I believe that the flow of God's power is not even close to that of the first church. I mean, let's be honest about the church of today; we know the Word of God like the back of our hand, but where is the manifestation of the power of God as it was in the first church? Are we the ones that God was talking about when he said,

*"Having **a form of godliness**, but denying the power thereof: from such turn away. 1ˢᵗ Timothy 3:5*

When was the last time you saw your pastor walk by the sick and they received their healing by simply being in the shadow of the man of God (Acts 5:15)? Exactly as I thought, it has not happened. Oh sure some are healed, some are baptized by the Holy Spirit and speak in tongues or prophesy, but we have not seen anything that can remotely come close to the power of God's Spirit demonstrated by the first Church. Jesus said, *"And greater works then these will he do" (John 14:12* speaking of those who believe. This is why you hear everyone screaming for Revival all the time because of the lack of power demonstrated; but think about it, Revival means to awaken or bring back from a state of unconsciousness. Does this mean that the church of today is asleep or in a condition that is equal to being in slumber? We would not need a Revival if we were living everyday according to the "True" purpose of the church. The unspoken rule here is that you don't have to awaken a church with Revival unless we are all asleep!!!

If I have learned anything about being a Christian, it is that if we are to expect anything from God it requires some type of action on our part because faith without works is dead faith! We all know that without faith it is impossible to please God. Well, giving is true faith because when you give, you are not supposed to look for anything in return! Tithing according to the church of today is too simple; you just give ten percent of your gross and sit back awaiting for God to pour it out on you. This concept is one of the reasons why so many people are suffering financially and spiritually. They think that tithing is all it takes to have a relationship with God!

Once, I was away from home on a temporary assignment while I was in the military. I went into a snack bar to get something to drink, and while the cashier was ringing up my order, I asked her, "Do you attend church anywhere?" With a justifying look, she responded with, "Sometimes I do but I always pay my Tithes!" This may sound like a faithful Tither to you, but to me it sounds like a person who is very mixed up. The Tithe has been pounded into people's heads so much that they know of nothing else concerning the blessings of God. They think that by putting the principle of Tithing in action they are in good standing with God, and thus they can still receive from him, HOGWASH! I'm here to tell you that if you don't know Jesus Christ as your personal, daily Savior, the blessings of God are passing you by and whatever you are receiving is nothing more than a mere illusion of the truth. In the book of Hebrews, chapter 7, verses 1-28, it shows us how.

> *The LAW made men with infirmity's high priest and how Jesus the son of God which cannot sympathize with our infirmities; but was in all points tempted like as we are, yet without sinning.*

You see, Jesus is the perfect system for men in whom we can be made righteous and holy before God. The ways of the LAW could not; it only pointed out and covered up sin. Therefore, our salvation comes from our obedience under the New Covenant and not the Old. We need to really concentrate on what Jesus told us to do and not on what bits and pieces of the LAW say. Remember, in the previous chapters, we discussed how Abraham paid tithes and he also circumcised his entire house. This was done well before the Law of Moses and is always pointed out when discussing the Tithe. But both of these practices, whether started before the Law or not, were made a very big part of the Law of Moses! We also looked at how Paul specifically noted that whether circumcised or not, the plan of salvation was for everyone.

Therefore, it is evident that if circumcision were not relevant, then neither would be the Tithe!

What is God's plan for us to receive our blessings? Is it for us to do what Malachi 3:10 says? That God wants us to Tithe and he will open up the windows of heaven and pour us out a blessing that there shall not be room enough to receive it? Looking at the teachings of Christ, as well as the intent of the Tithe, we see that it is our willingness to give that dictates what we shall receive. Whether our giving is of time, or money, or self, it all boils down to our love for God's Word (Jesus)! The question of how badly do we want whatever it is that God has in store for us is not relevant! Our true focus should be on being obedient, and then the blessings will flow. One Sunday morning during the sermon at my church, my pastor had a prophetic word come forth that during the upcoming years God will no longer give out handouts. That we as members of the Body of Christ are going to really have to truly trust and believe God for any and everything that we want. Now, to me, that is a no-brainer. But in lieu of this, it simply means that it is time for us to take our faith off of the closet shelf, dust it off, and put it to use like God intended it to be used! Paul said in Romans 12:3,

> *God hath dealt to every man "THE" measure of faith.*

The word "THE" used here represents that certain amount of faith that God has given to each of us so that no one can say they do not have enough faith. All we have to do is exercise "THE" measure of faith given to us so that it will develop and grow. You ask, how do we exercise our faith? It's simple; first you must study the word of God because,

> *Faith cometh by hearing, and hearing by the word of God.* Romans 10:17

Then we must ask the Holy Spirit to use us by placing us in situations so that we can be used. We have to get out there in the community and let our light shine. The only problem with doing this is that we have become so passive, so lazy, and so content that we would rather not use our faith but use that of someone else! How many times have you heard or maybe even asked someone yourself to pray for you because you don't have enough faith to believe God for yourself? Jesus told us in Mark 11:24,

> *Therefore I say unto you, what things soever*
> *ye desire, when ye pray, believe that ye*
> *receive them, and ye shall have them.*

Hey, isn't that receiving blessings? If you would simply put "THE" measure of faith that God has so generously given you to work sometimes, then you would know that you have the same ability as any other Holy Spirit-filled believer! Have you ever noticed that it's the same people getting in line for prayer all of the time? If I were a betting man, I would say that their requests for prayer are also the same thing over, and over, and over again! In Luke 6:38 Jesus tells us of not only how we can put our faith to work but also what the plan of God is for us to receive our blessings.

> *Give, and it shall be given unto you; good*
> *measure, pressed down and shaken together,*
> *and running over, SHALL MEN GIVE INTO*
> *YOUR BOSOM. For with the same measure*
> *that ye mete withal it shall be measured to*
> *you again.*

Why didn't Jesus say, *Tithe and it shall be Tithed unto you*? He did not say that because Tithing is no longer God's plan for the blessings to come upon his people. I know that change is not comfortable, and old habits are hard to let go of, but it is so very important that we open our hearts and minds and listen to what the spirit of God is telling us! A "Tradition of Men" can also stem from the

Bible itself, and we must be careful! As Christians we must understand the differences between how the Children of Israel followed God and how Christians are to follow Christ. As we have already established by studying the Scriptures, the Tithe is not practiced today like it was originally done anyway. So how can we even think that "IT" will determine our blessings? This way of Tithing that is practiced today is not done according to the way God established it under the LAW; therefore, how can we expect the promise of the Tithe, which was indeed under the LAW as well as the promised curses? On the other hand, Jesus' plan that was given to you and I as the New Covenant people of God incorporates the love of Christ by sharing and giving to others with the promised return of the same. Not only did Jesus say if you give it will be given unto you, but he also said,

> *It will be of good measure, pressed down,*
> *shaken together, and running over, shall men*
> *give unto your bossom.*

WOW, THAT'S GOOD! Can you imagine giving to someone or some cause, and God supernaturally taking what you have given, placing it through this system that Jesus explained and it comes back to you running over? If you ask me, this is even better than the windows of heaven opening up, because with Jesus Christ, instead of having an occasional open window, we have an eternal doorway to the kingdom of heaven. A doorway that will never close to those that believe, receive and obey him and his commandments.

Remember our discussion of Malachi? Remember how the windows of Heaven were closed to them because of the proclaimed curses of Moses' day? We saw that God was simply telling the people in Malachi that he would open the windows again for them if they returned unto him. Please do not lose focus of that even if you need to stop reading at this very moment and re-read it to yourself! In the past so many pastors have become addicted to and dependent on the Tithe that they no longer rely on God to meet their financial needs. In the few cases where they do rely on him, they limit him to making the congregation Tithe in order to keep their financial independence. Well, those days are over! No longer will leaders of the Body of Christ hold a curse from the LAW over their fellow, washed in the blood, redeemed from the curse of the LAW, sanctified, spirit-filled Christian's heads!

Notice in the book of Mark, chapter 12:41-44, how Jesus was watching the people put money into the treasury. Listen to what he said about the women who **gave** in comparison to the others.

> *And Jesus sat one against the treasury and beheld how the people cast money into the treasury and many that were rich cast in much. And there came a certain poor widow and she threw in two mites which make a farthling and he called unto him his disciples and saith unto them, verily I say unto you, that this poor widow hath cast more in than all they which have cast into the treasury: for all they did cast in of their abundance; but she of her WANT did cast in ALL that she had, even ALL her living.*

This woman had a want or a need that she knew God would meet, so she gave him everything that she had to show him her faith. She did not do as the others did and just give a certain part of what she had; she gave her best—she gave her ALL! God wants us to give him our ALL as well! Why didn't Jesus say to her, "Woman, you have put in too much money; you don't have anything to survive on! Here, take back ninety percent of what you placed in the treasury! You are only required to give ten percent and God the Father will bless you based on your Tithe"? Don't take what I'm saying the wrong way; I'm not telling you that you have to give everything that you own away, but what I'm telling you is that you must give God your best in everything that you do for the kingdom of God and that requires your faith—not just 10%, but 100%.

"How Did the First Church Do It?"

Let me ask you a question, what if we were supposed to give everything to the ministering of the kingdom? Could you give up everything that you own and love for the work of God? Remember, Matthew 6:21 says,

> *For where your treasure is, there will your heart be also.*

Maybe we need to do some self-checking on our hearts? This idea of giving everything is not so farfetched; in fact, this is exactly what the First Church did. Let's take a look at the book of Acts, starting at the second chapter, verses 41 through 47.

> *Then they that gladly received his word were baptized: and the same day there were added unto them about three thousand souls. And they continued steadfastly in the apostles' doctrine and fellowship, and in breaking of bread, and in prayers. And fear came upon every soul: and many wonders and signs were done by the apostles. And all that believed were together, and had all things common; and SOLD THEIR POSSESSIONS AND GOODS, AND PARTED THEM TO ALL MEN, AS EVERY MAN HAD NEED. And they, continuing daily with one accord in the temple, and breaking bread from HOUSE TO HOUSE, did eat their meat with gladness and singleness of heart, Praising God, and having*

*favor with all the people. And the Lord added
to the church daily such as should be saved.*

Now that is what I call being in this world and not of
this world. If you were to start preaching this, people would
automatically say that you are trying to create some type of
cult, but regardless of what someone may think or say, this is
the way the Bible depicts the first church. They preached the
message of the Gospel of Jesus Christ; people were saved;
no one was sick among them; they visited and ministered
from house to house, and the Lord, the same Lord that you
and I serve, added to them daily. You want to know why?
Because all that believed were together and they had all
things in common. You want to know another reason the
Lord added to them daily? Because they were all focused on
the one thing that Jesus taught them and that was "Love thy
neighbor as thy self." By obeying this commandment, they
had no problem selling things of their own in order to help
their brothers. By loving their neighbor they had no problem
going from house to house ministering to the lost. It was all
done out of love for God's word and love for their fellow
man.

This is why the Lord blessed them and added to them
daily, because of their obedience to his commandments. (Oh,
by the way, did you happen to notice the tithe mentioned
anywhere in their financial agenda?) So many of us feel like
we can just pay ten percent of our money and that's it. Well,
I hate to be the bearer of bad news, but if all you can do for
God is to give him ten percent, then that's probably exactly
what you will receive! Throughout America and the world,
the church is preaching it all the time that we walk by faith
and not by sight, but are we ready to really live by what we
preach? You see, God created the Tithe for the Children of
Israel to show God how grateful they were toward him, and
to provide for the Priest, not for the Tithe to take God's place
as their provider. Today, the Tithe is the source for the
church to survive in their financial endeavors. If we are
looking at the Tithe as our source, then we truly need to seek

God, our true source, and ask for his forgiveness. Remember what Paul said to the Romans in 1:25, about the people who rebelled against God's word; Paul said,

> *Who changed the truth of God into a lie, and worshipped and served the CREATURE more than the CREATOR.*

The next time some man is ramping and raging over the church not Tithing, instead of teaching what Jesus said, ask yourself this question, who do we serve and who are we depending on, GOD THE CREATOR, or THE TITHE A CREATION OF GOD? Now, I want to show you one more illustration of how the principle of Tithing under the LAW was transferred and changed into the principle of Giving. As we have seen in our study of the first church, we can safely say that they practiced the commandment to give. Looking at the Commandment to Tithe, we see that every year you would Tithe the increase of your field and your herds. You were also required to take out of that and give it unto the people that were in need, but at the end of three years, you were required to place your entire Tithe at your gates (or at the entrance to your land). Now, how many churches that practice the Tithe insist that their members participate in this three-year Tithe that you know of?

This was for the people that were in need, to come and eat of it all (SEE DEUTERONOMY 14:22-29). As you can see out of the act of obedience to the Three-Year Tithe, God wanted the Children of Israel to help those in need by using the entire Tithe! Now, I know that really messes with a lot of folks' theology, but this is the Word of God. This principle behind the Three-Year Tithe is incorporated in Giving, but most ministers will mix the two by saying "Tithes, Offerings and your Giving." To illustrate further exactly what Jesus taught the Disciples to teach to us, let's look at what Paul taught about the purpose of Giving. In 2 Corinthians, chapter 8, verses 10 through 15, Paul writes,

And herein I give my advice: for this is profitable for you, who have begun before, not only to do, and were desiring to do a year ago. But now you also must complete the doing of it; that as there was a readiness to will, so there may be a completion also out of that which ye have. For if there be first a willing mind, it is accepted according to that a man hath, and not according to that he hath not. FOR I MEAN NOT THAT OTHER MEN BE EASED, AND YE BURDENED: BUT BY AND EQUALITY, THAT NOW AT THIS TIME YOUR ABUNDANCE MAY BE A SUPPLY FOR THEIR LACK, THAT THEIR ABUNDANCE ALSO MAY BE A SUPPLY FOR YOUR LACK: THAT THERE MAY BE EQUALITY: As it is written, HE THAT HAD GATHERED MUCH HAD NOTHING OVER; AND HE THAT HAD GATHERED LITTLE HAD NO LACK.

Now, we know from our previous studies that Jesus would often use the commandments of old to illustrate things to the Disciples. This very Scripture used by Paul is a direct quote from the book of Exodus 16:18, where Moses instructed the Children of Israel to go out and gather twice the amount of bread on the sixth day in preparation for the Sabbath day lock-in. The bread would be used for everyone's substance, even for those that had nothing. The Commandment to Give incorporates this same principle of Giving in that everyone's need will be met. Paul tells us in verse 13,

For I mean not that other men be eased, and ye burdened: But by an equality, that now at this time your ABUNDANCE may be a SUPPLY FOR THEIR LACK, that their ABUNDANCE also be a SUPPLY FOR YOUR LACK: that there may be equality.

You see it all actually goes back to the First Church and how they provided the Church then with their finances and substance. To give you an illustration of how this worked, let's say that you had a church of 100 people. Out of the 100 members, 50 of them had $100, which gave you a total of $5,000.00. The other 50 members only had $50, which equaled $2,500.00, giving your treasury a total of $7,500.00. Now, what you would do, being the leader of that church, would be to distribute the money to every person as they had need. This required total communication and honesty between everyone. One might have a total amount of bills, let's say, equaling $40 and another person might have a total amount of bills of $70. Both members would have their bills paid, money for food, and as it is stated in verse 15, *As it is written, He that had GATHERED MUCH had NOTHING OVER; and he that had GATHERED LITTLE had NO LACK.*

So as you can see, the two concepts (The Three Year Tithe and Giving) are the same in that the outcome is everyone having all things in common, and there is nothing standing in the way of the ministry. Now, concerning the Finances for the ministering of the gospel, the church of today has quickly picked that up. As we study the ministry of our Lord, we see how after he prepared them he would send them out two by two so that they could minister to people and prepare the way for Christ. Later on, after Jesus ascended, the Disciples continued this practice of sending men out by twos to go and minister to people all around. But notice how before they went out, they were prepared! Most churches don't even send their top leadership out, let alone the members, but this is the root of the problem in today's religious system! If we were at least focused on our true mission as the first church was, then many of our problems would not exist. Paul talks about the Giving that the different churches did and how by their giving to support the ministry, God will reward them. What? Giving plus God rewarding them for their Giving? Is that another blessing I see? 2 Corinthians, chapter 9 reads,

> *For as touching the ministering to the saints, it is superfluous for me to write to you: For I know the willingness of your mind, for which I boast of you to them of Mac'-e-do'-ni-a, that A-cha'-ia was ready a year ago; and your zeal hath stirred up the majority. Yet have I sent the brethren, lest our boasting of you should be in vain in this behalf; that, as I said, ye may be ready: Lest haply if they of Mac-e-do'-ni-a come with me, and find you unprepared, we not to mention you should be ashamed in this same confident boasting. Therefore I thought it necessary to exhort the brethren, that they would go on ahead unto you, and make up beforehand your bountiful gift, whereof ye had promised before, that the same might be ready, as a matter of GENEROSITY, and not as of GRUDGING OBLIGATION.*

You see, Paul is writing in this portion of his letter about how he has spoken highly of the church at this particular location. He is sending someone ahead of himself, so they can help prepare this particular group, of the Body of Christ, to Give their gift to Paul for the ministering of the gospel. Not only did Paul send him to help them with their Giving, but also to help them Give out of the right spirit. That is why in verse 5 he said, *"That the same might be ready, as a matter of GENEROSITY, and not as of GRUDGING OBLIGATION"*. As mentioned earlier, the Body of Christ today has indeed picked up on this in that some members travel the world and minister to others. They hold different types of fundraisers to aid in their calling, but many times they still come up short. This is why we should take another look at this and come together to accomplish the Great Commission that Jesus gave us. Not one or two people can do it alone, but it is going to take the entire Body of Christ as a whole to lay down our individuality, our own beliefs, and our denominational boundaries, which are all man made! I don't care if you are Catholic, Protestant, Baptist, Pentecostal, Church of Christ, Seven Day Adventist, or Lutheran—it is time that we obey the Scriptures.

> *"For ye are all one in Christ Jesus".*
> Galatians 3:28

We must come to grips on what the spirit of God is saying to us. In verses 6 through 8, we see Paul capping off this lesson on Giving by explaining the Principles and promised blessings of being obedient; he writes,

> *But this I say, He which soweth sparingly shall reap also sparingly; and he which soweth in blessings shall reap also blessings. Every man according as he purposeth in his heart, so let him give; not grudgingly, or of compulsion: for God loveth a CHEERFUL GIVER. And God is able to make all grace abound toward you; that ye, always having all sufficiency in all things, may abound to every good work: (As it is written, He hath dispersed abroad; he hath given to the poor: his righteousness remaineth for ever.)*

Once again, I hate to mess with one's theology, but Paul did not mention the Tithe at all; however, he did mention the blessings!

Note from the Author

I hope that by reading this book and by studying the Scriptures for YOURSELF that your eyes have been opened. To the ministers of the gospel that preach and teach the Tithe, I am neither attacking you nor would I condemn you for your understanding and interpretation of the Scripture. I do pray that the Holy Spirit—that precious spirit of the Living God—will reveal the truth and you will realize that we no longer have to live under a curse from the LAW. Jesus Christ has already become a curse for you and I, so give him praise and glory for all of his wonderful acts and his Holy name! Grace and peace be unto you from God the Father and our Lord Jesus Christ.

CPSIA information can be obtained at www.ICGtesting.com
Printed in the USA
LVOW042313200911

247160LV00001B/145/A